THE MORAL FOUNDATIONS OF EDUCATIONAL RESEARCH

Knowledge, Inquiry and Values

THE MORAL FOUNDATIONS OF EDUCATIONAL RESEARCH

Knowledge, Inquiry and Values

Edited by Pat Sikes, Jon Nixon and Wilfred Carr

Open University Press
Maidenhead · Philadelphia

Open University Press
McGraw-Hill Education
McGraw-Hill House
Shoppenhangers Road
Maidenhead
Berkshire
England
SL6 2QL

email: enquiries@openup.co.uk
world wide web: www.openup.co.uk

and
325 Chestnut Street
Philadelphia, PA 19106, USA

First Published 2003

A catalogue record of this book is available from the British Library

ISBN 0 335 21046 5 (pb) 0 335 21100 3 (hb)

Library of Congress Cataloging-in-Publication Data
The moral foundations of educational research: knowledge, inquiry, and values/edited by Pat Sikes, Jon Nixon, and Wilfred Carr.
p. cm.
Includes bibliographical references and index.
ISBN 0-335-21100-3 – ISBN 0-335-21046-5 (pbk.)
1. Education–Research–Moral and ethical aspects. I. Sikes, Patricia J. II. Nixon, Jon. III. Carr, Wilfred.
LB1028.M6433 2003
370'.7'2–dc21 2002074954

Typeset by Type Study, Scarborough
Printed in Great Britain by Biddles Ltd, *www.biddles.co.uk*

Contents

Introduction: reconceptualizing the debate 1
Jon Nixon and Pat Sikes

1 Educational research and its histories 6
Wilfred Carr

2 Towards a social history of educational research 18
Gary McCulloch

3 Living research: thoughts on educational research as moral practice 32
Pat Sikes and Ivor Goodson

4 The virtues and vices of an educational researcher 52
Richard Pring

5 Against objectivism: the reality of the social fiction 68
Pierre Bourdieu

6 Research as thoughtful practice 86
Jon Nixon, Melanie Walker and Peter Clough

7 On goodness and utility in educational research 105
Carrie Paechter

8 Method and morality: practical politics and the science of human affairs 118
Fred Inglis

Biographical notes on contributors 134

Introduction: reconceptualizing the debate

Jon Nixon and Pat Sikes

The discussions from which this book has developed were a direct response to the changing pattern of doctoral research within which 'research training' is now seen as an essential component. The editors of this book were centrally involved in translating recent policy directives emanating, in particular, from the Economic and Social Research Council (ESRC) into a coherent programme of doctoral study for use within the School of Education, University of Sheffield. The proposed pattern of four-year doctoral study, with a first-year stand-alone element focusing on methodological issues, necessitated some serious thinking as to what constitutes an adequate preparation for doctoral study and, indeed, for any independent inquiry within the field of educational research.

The most cursory of literature searches reveals a significant expansion over the past ten years in the publication of books on methodological issues within the social sciences generally and educational research in particular. Major publishing houses have developed whole series devoted precisely to this policy agenda. Although much of what is being written is useful and challenging, most focuses on particular approaches to educational research and the specific techniques of data gathering and analysis associated with these broad approaches. 'Method', it seemed to us, was being pluralized before being grasped in its conceptual singularity. What seemed to us to be lacking was any sustained attempt to address what is distinctive about educational research. There is little in the literature to suggest that it is anything other than just a conglomeration of techniques borrowed from the social sciences and applied to educational settings.

That, in the main, seems to be the prevailing view. What distinguishes educational research, according to this view, is its 'usefulness' and 'relevance' to those working in educational settings. We do not argue with this emphasis on the generation of 'useful' and 'relevant' knowledge, but would suggest that whatever it is that is educational about educational research requires a fuller and more rounded explanation: an explanation that takes cognisance of the educational purposefulness of educational research and the moral values of those who conduct it. Educational research is grounded, epistemologically, in the moral foundations of educational practice. It is the epistemological and moral purposes underlying the 'usefulness' and 'relevance' of educational research that matter.

So, methodology starts, for us, not with the widely endorsed (and, indeed, irrefutable) claim that educational research should be 'useful' and 'relevant', but with the attempt to justify and elaborate that claim with reference to its historical precedents. 'Usefulness' and 'relevance' are not simply a matter of impact and influence; they involve a radical reconceptualization of what is *educationally* worthwhile in what we deem to be 'useful' and 'relevant'. (The attempt to develop the educational means of achieving ends that are not educationally worthwhile is, as R.S. Peters warned, not only suspect but potentially dangerous.) It is to the history of educational thought that we return to reclaim the moral and epistemological foundations of our discipline.

We began, then, with a practical problem and a hunch. Our hunch was that to think methodologically we needed to think educationally. At the time, Wilfred Carr was Head of the School of Education at the University of Sheffield and it was on his initiative that what might have been a simple exercise in course development became an intellectually challenging and collegial exercise in rethinking the foundations of educational research: an exercise, it should be emphasized, that is still in process. He found the necessary funding to hold two invited seminars, led by Pat Sikes, at which the contributors were able to share ideas and at which Professor Anne Edwards of the University of Birmingham and Professor Martyn Hammersley of The Open University made valuable, and in the case of Professor Hammersley, critical contributions. Those contributions were greatly appreciated.

The work of Professor Pierre Bourdieu was a highly significant reference point in our deliberations regarding the ends and purposes of educational research. Although Professor Bourdieu was unable to attend our seminars, he gave permission for his work to be represented in this volume in the form of an edited extract from one of his recent works. Fred Inglis volunteered to undertake the task of producing this chapter and of corresponding with Professor Bourdieu on matters relating to its form and content. Professor Bourdieu's death deprives us of the opportunity to pursue this particular dialogue. However, as Professor Inglis's foreword to Bourdieu's chapter makes clear, his legacy will live on in our deliberations and aspirations and in our various intellectual histories.

This, then, is both a reconstructive and deconstructive text. The contributors are concerned not only with critiquing the current understanding of educational research, but also with signalling the kinds of reorientations necessary to mount such a critique. Those reorientations involve, crucially, a historical reassessment of the role and purposes of educational research, with a view to making explicit its moral and epistemological assumptions.

Notwithstanding the very real differences – of perspective, value and intellectual background – between the contributors to this volume, they agree that what is required is not yet another methodological innovation, but a sustained and purposeful consideration of what constitutes educational research. They agree, also, that only through an examination of the traditions and practices of educational research can that kind of consideration become a possibility.

An historical analysis of the provenance and authority of educational research is, therefore, a major element in the very different analyses developed in the following chapters. Carr traces what he terms 'the two histories of educational research': a Whig interpretation of history that reads the past in terms of the present and a Hegelian interpretation of history that reads the present in terms of the past. He argues that these two histories provide very different interpretations of the nature of educational research and that these interpretations, in turn, produce rival and often incompatible methodologies and perspectives. McCulloch reframes that analysis through a close reading of the social/historical context of educational research. His major concern is in tracing that history in relation to the broader field of educational studies as it has developed over the last fifty years. Educational studies and educational research, he argues, are bound together historically, but constitute an epistemological 'bind': the history he traces is one of tension and contradiction, not one of smooth development and transition.

Sikes and Goodson ground their historical deliberation in the contradictions of their own career paths as educational researchers. In doing so, they shift the emphasis from the epistemological to the ethical. They argue that life history, as a form of educational research, has the reflexive potential for reconciling the historical and structural contradictions highlighted in the previous analyses. They are concerned with the complex relation between origins and beginnings, conditions and capacities, constraints and possibilities. Pring pursues this line of moral argument through a discussion of codes of ethical conduct in relation to the practice of educational research. Drawing a distinction between rules and principles, he argues that the latter can only be understood in terms of the virtues of those who espouse them. The espousal of principle gains authenticity through the practice of virtue.

Bourdieu brings together these various historical, epistemological and ethical strands in his oppositional meditation against crude objectivism. Implicated as we are, as educational researchers, in the complexities of our object of study, we must seek a radically new conceptualization of the relation between subject and object. Our dispositions are shaped by, and shape, the field within which we pursue our enquiries. Bourdieu invites us to render our subjectivities objective; to participate through the practice of research in a process of rigorous reflexivity whereby dispositions, and the fields within which dispositions achieve authenticity, are called to account. Bourdieu sought a theoretically precise – and, therefore, necessarily difficult

– language with which to reconcile what he saw as the false dichotomy of objectivity versus subjectivity. He worried away at the paradox whereby social reality is only objective by virtue of our inter-subjectivity.

Nixon, Walker and Clough seek to instantiate this synthesis of historical, epistemological and ethical concerns through an elaboration of what they term 'thoughtful research'. They are centrally concerned with the relation between thought and action: What makes action thoughtful? What gives thought its agency? They address these questions through readings of three very different research accounts, and conclude with some tentative suggestions as to what might constitute thoughtful research. Paechter provides another way forward through her discussion of what she calls 'deconstructive research', by which she means research that is committed to questioning the assumptions underlying the discourses and practices of education. She is particularly concerned with questioning the relation between goodness and utility in educational research: Is good research necessarily useful? Is useful research necessarily good? Wherein lies goodness?

Inglis, in the final chapter of the book, reminds us that whatever meaning we make of educational research is premised on whatever meaning we make of educational practice in all its diversity. He also reminds us that the meanings we make are unmistakably moral matters. He suggests that the morality of educational research lies in our capacity to transgress the precept that we should only address questions that have some prospect of being answered. It is not the esoteric, but the customary and the ordinary, that confronts us with the seemingly unanswerable questions. These, Inglis argues, are the only questions worth addressing: the only worthwhile questions for those who take seriously the moral charge and potential of educational research.

Readers will come to this book with their own requirements. We hope, however, that it will prompt them to reflect upon what it is they are doing when they conduct, read or sponsor educational research. In particular, we would ask our readers (whether research students, experienced researchers or 'users' of research) to bear in mind the following points:

- Educational research is not just research *about* education, but research with an educational purpose. It requires of its practitioners the willingness to ask themselves what is educational about educational research. We think that, in addressing that question, there is an overriding need not only to define research method in technical terms, but to make explicit its educational rationale.
- We also think that the distinction between substantive and methodological concerns is more complex than it may seem. The consideration of method begins with a long and reasoned absorption in the conceptualization of the research problem. Method is never simply a means to an end, but is always implicit in the horizons set by the intellectual project it serves.

- Research is from the outset, and throughout, a process of conceptualization. There are no ready-made problems, no ready-made methods, no ready-made frameworks of analysis. There are traditions and practices, but these must be reworked and rethought in the creative endeavour that constitutes educational research. Indeed, that is the only way in which the traditions and practices are renewed.

Methodology is centrally concerned with method. But method cannot be reduced to technique. Method rules, and is ruled by, the myriad adjustments, accommodations and resistances that constitute our being together. Method is a matter of history and morality, both of which inform and prescribe the epistemological assumptions underlying its application. To study method – to do methodology – is to render those assumptions transparent and open to critical scrutiny. This book invites its readers – research students, fellow researchers, scholars and, we would hope, policy makers and practitioners – to rethink the bases of educational research and, in so doing, to reconsider their own ends and purposes within the broad field of educational studies.

Each of the contributions to this volume presents the reader with a different kind of 'difficulty', because each in its own way is challenging dominant presuppositions regarding the nature of methodological thought. Facility is to be admired, but not when it masks what is facile – as it so often does in the kind of technical compendia that masquerade as methodology. For all their occasional 'difficulty', the following essays are prompted by the democratic impulse towards transparency and openness. They are – and should be read as – attempts by their authors to go on learning about what it is they are doing when they do research, and to communicate that learning to others. They seek to reclaim methodology from the specialist margins of technical discourse and to relocate it within the broad mainstream of educational thought and practice. 'Education is ordinary', as Raymond Williams famously declared, but explaining why 'ordinariness' matters is an extraordinarily difficult task.

We want to emphasize that the following essays in methodological thinking are only a beginning. They do not provide a comprehensive overview of the methodology of educational research. They do, however, provide a starting point from which the usual topics of methodological debate might follow: the technicalities of how to collect evidence, how to analyse it, how to report it, and so on. Our point is that these topics, which are so often seen as the defining parameters of the methodological debate, are secondary to the primary concern with why, educationally, we do what we do in the way in which we do it. In addressing that concern, we must acknowledge the moral foundations of educational research and the ways in which our own values rest upon, and sometimes resist, those foundations.

1 | Educational research and its histories

Wilfred Carr

He who cannot draw on three thousand
years is living from hand to mouth.

Goethe

Introduction

Educational research is in a state of crisis in two specific ways. First, educational researchers appear unable to provide any coherent or convincing answers to the critical questions that are now being asked by their external critics about what educational research is for and how its achievements are to be measured. Unless and until it can produce a more cogent justification for its existence, educational research will continue to display all the characteristics of an endangered species hovering on the verge of extinction. Second, but not entirely unrelated to this external threat, there is now a conspicuous absence of any internal agreement about 'what educational research is' that can command anything remotely resembling universal assent. Educational researchers may behave as if they constitute a unified academic community, but the sad truth is that they now employ so many rival, and often incompatible, paradigms, methodologies and perspectives, that whatever identity educational research may claim to possess stems more from its institutional embodiment in university departments, conferences and journals than from its intellectual unity.

What I want to suggest in this chapter is that this state of affairs cannot be rectified simply by making minor modifications to the established *status quo*. Indeed, what distinguishes the argument running through this chapter is the conviction that the various criticisms now being made of educational research are the entirely predictable manifestation of some of the dubious assumptions deeply embedded in the self-understanding in terms of which most educational researchers make what they do intelligible to themselves and others, and which allows them to make sense of their educational and cultural role. It follows from this that any serious discussion of the kind of difficulties that now confront educational research can only proceed if we are prepared to re-examine the understanding of educational research embedded in current conventions and practice. It also follows that this kind of re-examination can only be undertaken by first adopting an external vantage point that allows us to transcend the boundaries of our present understanding of educational research and so make this understanding itself an object for critical reflection. In other words, what any serious examination of the current state of educational research requires is a new level of methodological self-consciousness that would enable educational researchers to be more critically aware of the preconceptions governing their own understanding of what they do and what they are trying to achieve. What would the development of this new level of methodological self-consciousness require?

What, initially, it would require is an admission of how, because of a general diffidence to its own history, educational research had deprived itself of any adequate understanding of its relationship to its own past and hence of that form of historical self-consciousness necessary to sustain some sense of how educational research emerged and why it has developed in the way that it has. Thus, what the development of this new level of methodological self-consciousness would require is an historical narrative that shows how our present understanding of educational research originated, how it evolved under certain historical conditions and how it has become embedded in the structures and institutions within which educational research is now conducted. However, since the point and purpose of this historical inquiry is to allow us critically to reconsider our current understanding of what educational research is, to write it as a history of what is currently understood as education research would be to presuppose an answer to the very question such an inquiry was supposed to address. One way of avoiding this kind of question-begging circularity would be to produce a second historical narrative that relativizes the historical reconstruction of our present understanding of educational research by interpreting it as no more than the latest episode in a much larger and longer history of evolution and change. In other words, transcending the limitations and inadequacies of our present understanding of educational research would require not one history of educational research but two. How, in general terms, would these two histories be written?

The two histories of educational research

The first of these histories would offer the kind of Whig interpretation of history that treats the past as a mere prelude to the present. From this perspective, the history of educational research would give an account of the achievements and developments through which educational research has progressively advanced to become the kind of modern academic profession that it now is. So understood, the history of educational research would be a species of British social history designed to reveal how the major social changes and achievements of the nineteenth century – industrialization, the introduction of mass schooling, the growth of science and the emergence of the liberal democratic state – led to the creation of what we now call educational research. It would, therefore, bear some resemblance to Philip Abrams' (1968) historical study of the growth of social research: *The Origins of British Sociology 1834–1914*.

Two features of the nineteenth-century political and social context would provide the broad backcloth against which this history would be written. The first would be the widespread concern that dominated political debate in the first half of the century: the desperate social and economic conditions of the new labouring classes created in the aftermath of the Industrial Revolution. What this history would emphasize is how, within this debate, social and educational reform was advanced because it was seen as an important instrument for combating the problems of social order and civil unrest that had been created by industrialization and urbanization. What, in particular, this history would show is that those advancing the case for social and educational reform did so, not because of any strong desire to improve the well-being of the working class, but because they believed that the best way to resist threats to the existing social order was to provide working-class children with an elementary education that would instil in them the knowledge, values and attitudes that would reconcile them to their future social and economic roles in the emerging industrial society. What, in short, this history would make abundantly clear is that the impetus for educational and social reform was not social change but social control.

The second general feature of the nineteenth-century political climate that such a history would need to stress would be the extent to which the existing social order was legitimized by the political philosophy of classical liberalism. Two features of this philosophy were to influence what was to count as politically acceptable solutions to the social problems created by industrial capitalism and hence the kinds of social and educational reforms that eventually emerged. The first was its excessive individualism, which legitimized the fear that state-provision of social and educational services would replace self-reliance by state dependency and eventually lead to an infringement of personal liberty. The second was its utilitarianism: its insistence that the contribution of any public institution to the common good had to be calculated in terms of its productive usefulness. When combined with the *laissez-faire* economic doctrines of the time, this inevitably led to the assumption that the criteria for judging any state-provided social and welfare services were their effectiveness and efficiency and that the burden on the taxpayer should be kept as low as possible.

By the mid-1850s, the climate of opinion created by this kind of utilitarian thinking ensured that the 'problems' of education were defined in terms of two specific issues: the administrative problems of making the ever increasing number of state-funded schools accountable for the effectiveness of their work, and the economic problem of reducing the ever increasing Exchequer grants for education. To find solutions to these problems, the government set up The Newcastle Commission of 1858 to inquire into 'the Present State of Popular Education in England and to consider what measures are required for the extension of sound and cheap Elementary Education'. In its report of 1861, the Commission famously recommended as solutions to these problems a system of 'payment by results', which was designed to ensure that all pupils in elementary schools should be educated as effectively and as cheaply as possible.

The importance of the Newcastle Report for this history of educational research is that it was the first government body to commission extensive surveys to provide statistical data about the adequacy of existing elementary school provision across the country. In this sense, the Newcastle Commission reflected not only the Victorian response to the pressures for social and economic reform, but also the widespread belief that any reform legislation had to be based on a systematic body of knowledge and information. This belief found public and institutional expression with the formation in 1856 of the National Association for the Promotion of Social Science (NAPSS), an organization that was to have a major influence on the subsequent development of educational research.

The NAPSS was an umbrella organization dedicated to promoting social reform through the scientific study of society and its institutions. Under the charter of the association, various social reform groups began to study state schooling not as a disinterested topic of study, but because it was believed that education would help to eliminate moral depravity and so reduce the threats to social order posed by an uneducated and hence potentially unruly working class. To this end, the association adopted a view of social science as having the essentially ameliorative function of finding remedies to social and educational problems that did not question the dominant liberal and utilitarian philosophies of the time. It is thus unsurprising that the studies of education conducted under the auspices of the NAPSS were limited to the study of state schooling and simply assumed that non-state education offered by the public and grammar schools was in good order. Nor is it surprising that the kind of 'social science' promoted by the association was an essentially theory-free enterprise dedicated to conducting large-scale statistical surveys – a research method that was subsequently extended and refined by Charles Booth in his seminal seventeen-volume study of *The Life and Labour of the People of London* (1902).

If this history of the nineteenth-century origins of educational research were to be spelt out in all its concrete detail, it would have to give serious attention to the late nineteenth-century efforts to establish a 'science of education' that could replicate the aims and methods of the natural sciences (Bain 1879). It would also need to make clear how the kind of educational research that originated in the nineteenth century provided, in embryonic form, a structure of assumptions and beliefs that still exercises a predominant influence on our understanding of the nature and purpose of educational research. Some of the assumptions and beliefs providing this historical continuity can be rapidly stated. One is that research is a branch of applied social research and, as such, a data-gathering activity that can be conducted without reference to any theoretical or conceptual scheme. Another is that, as a methodical and largely theory-free enterprise, educational research produces 'findings' through the systematic collection and analysis of factual data. Yet another is that essential to the reliability and validity of these 'findings' is the use of quantitative research methods in general and methods of statistical analysis in particular. What is also assumed is a utilitarian view of how research relates to policy and hence of how the relationship between educational research and educational change is to be understood. What, finally, has been inherited from the nineteenth century is a willingness to accept a politically defined research agenda that fails to acknowledge fully that many educational problems may be more fundamentally problematic than the political *status quo* would readily accept.

What this version of the history of educational research would show, then, is that despite the development of increasingly sophisticated methods and techniques, British educational research in the twentieth century has largely retained the distinctive features of applied social research it had acquired in the second half of the nineteenth century. One question this history may wish to consider is the extent to which the enduring strengths of nineteenth-century empiricism and positivism in twentieth-century English intellectual and cultural life helped to reinforce the continuing belief that the scientific study of education always proceeds through impartial observation and the disinterested collection of facts. Another would be the question of why educational research has not, to any significant extent, been influenced by theoretical developments in the academic social sciences. What, finally, such a history may wish to consider is how, as educational research has expanded into a professionalized specialism, so it has become increasingly regulated, managed and controlled through mechanisms that ensure that the continuity of the nineteenth-century understanding of educational research is sustained.

My second and very different history of educational research is not Whigish but Hegelian. It does not, therefore, simply abstract from the past those incidents and events that illuminate and explain educational research as it is presently understood. Instead, it insists that the past is never something to be discarded in favour of the present and that the future depends on transcending and correcting the limitations of our current understanding of educational research by transcending and correcting misunderstandings inherited from the past. From this perspective, the purpose of the history of educational research is not to provide a history of our current understanding of educational research, but an historical account that will help us to critically and reflectively transform our present understanding of what educational research is. From this perspective, the history of educational research is seen as a part of the history of education, which itself is seen as part of the general history of social evolution and change. It draws, therefore, on those histories of education such as David Hamilton's (1990) *Learning about Education* and Joan Simon's (1970) *The Social Origins of English Education*, which recognize the role of education in the development of human and social life.

The starting point for this history of educational research would be a Darwinian account of that period in the pre-history of *Homo sapiens* during which the human species, through the long slow development of the capacity for thought and language, gradually became less dependent on biologically transmitted instincts for its survival and began to acquire socially transmitted strategies for dealing with the environment that could be transmitted from generation to generation. Slowly, and imperceptibly, this capacity to learn from previous generations enabled the species to become less a passive product of its environment and more an active producer of its environment, shaping and controlling the natural world to its own needs. This, in turn, led to the creation of a social environment – or 'society' – in which human beings were no longer prisoners of the natural world. In such human societies, the processes of biological evolution and change began to be accompanied, and eventually superseded, by the processes of social evolution and change. As well as living in the natural world, human beings also lived in a social world which they themselves had created, which they themselves reproduced and which they themselves could transform and change.

As human beings became increasingly conscious of this process of social reproduction, so the need for new generations to learn more formally the rituals, rules, routines and conventions of social life became more obvious. They therefore developed a range of social practices by which children could be more systematically initiated into the shared understanding and mode of consciousness which provided the basis of the social life of the community. As the significance of these childrearing practices for the maintenance and continuity of social life became more apparent, so they gradually became more regulated and more culturally defined. Eventually, the task of socializing and enculturating new members of society itself became the distinctive and specialized cultural process we now call education – the process through which the way of life of a cultural community could be conserved, elaborated and transmitted to succeeding generations. In his book *Understanding Education*, the American educational philosopher Walter Feinberg (1983) outlines this view of education in the following way:

> To speak of education as social reproduction . . . is to recognise its primary role in maintaining intergenerational continuity and in maintaining the identity of a society across generations . . . At the most basic level, the study of education involves an analysis of the process whereby a society reproduces itself over time such that it can be said of one generation that it belongs to the same society as did generations long past and generations not yet born.
>
> (Feinberg 1983: 155)

In pre-literate, traditional societies, education was confined to uncritically transmitting the knowledge, understandings and skills that had to be handed down from generation to generation to maintain social continuity. However, as the intrinsic importance of education to the process of social reproduction became more self-consciously recognized, so too was its potential as an instrument of social transformation and change. It is thus unsurprising that when, in ancient Athens in the fourth century B.C., fundamental political questions began to emerge about the present condition and future shape of Athenian society, they became inseparable from practical educational questions about what should be taught and learned. One of the first to systematically and simultaneously confront these political and educational questions was Plato (428–347 B.C.), whose *Republic* still remains the most famous study of education ever written. What, in the *Republic*, Plato so clearly saw was how any educational inquiry always presupposes some inquiry into the nature of the 'good society' and how this always involves articulating the social, political and economic roles that individuals must be educated to perform if any vision of the 'good society' is to be realized and sustained. It is thus unsurprising that the *Republic* still serves as a paradigmatic example of an educational inquiry that acknowledges the pivotal role that education always plays in reproducing and transforming the political, cultural and economic life of a society.

Plato's *Republic* marked the emergence of a tradition of educational inquiry in which it is taken for granted that educational issues can only be examined and understood as aspects of the larger problems of society as it tries to come to terms with changing social conditions and cultural circumstances. Within this tradition of inquiry, the process of educational change cannot be understood or examined independently of the process of social change. Both are treated as mutually constitutive and dialectically related elements within the complex but single process of social evolution – the process through which both education and society are continuously and simultaneously reproduced and transformed.

The name given to this tradition of inquiry by Aristotle – Plato's most renowned pupil and heir – was 'practical philosophy', which, unlike 'theoretical philosophy', did not aim to discover 'truth', but instead sought to discover the nature of the good society and how it was to be realized. Aristotle characterized practical philosophy as an inexact science – a wide-ranging form of deliberative and reflective inquiry in which educational questions were always related to political and ethical questions about the 'good society', the kind of society that would best enable its members to live satisfying and worthwhile lives. Within this tradition, Plato's *Republic*, Rousseau's *Emile* and Dewey's *Democracy and Education* have acquired the status of canonical texts precisely because they articulate a morally compelling vision of the 'good society' and the role of education in its formation. Because the particular vision of the 'good society' advanced in each of these texts provides both the basis for a critique of an existing social order and the criteria against which educational proposals can be evaluated, it is hardly surprising that they treat questions about the aims, form and content of education and questions about what constitutes the 'good society' as interdependent. To engage in educational inquiry from within this tradition is thus not only to engage in argument with the architects of current educational policy, but also to participate in that historically extended dialogue in which questions about the kind of education that would promote a desirable form of social life are consciously addressed and in which the voices of Plato, Rousseau and Dewey have played a decisive role.

Up to and including the seventeenth century, this tradition of practical philosophy provided educational inquiry with its primary source of understanding and education, like politics, was interpreted as a species of those morally informed and ethically principled activities that Aristotle had called *praxis*. However, with the onset of modernity and the emergence of modern science, various new disciplines began to detach themselves from philosophy and declare themselves to be autonomous sciences. So, for example, in the age after Newton, natural science detached itself from metaphysics and natural philosophy. Similarly, in the age after Adam Smith, first political economy and then politics and economics became detached from moral and social philosophy.

In the context of this history of educational research, two related features of this process are worth noting. The first is how, by the middle of the nineteenth century, empirical forms of social inquiry began to emerge in response to the need to investigate a residue of questions that could find no place in practical philosophy – questions that themselves reflected the demands of society for solutions to the social problems caused by industrialization. Thus, the second is how the nineteenth-century expansion of a state-provided system of schooling made it imperative for traditional philosophical forms of educational inquiry to take a new depoliticized and non-theoretical form. For what the institutionalization of education into a system of schooling required was not a form of inquiry dedicated to the pursuit of the 'good society', but a form of inquiry that would focus on narrower administrative and technical issues about the effective regulation and reform of the newly emerging system of state schooling. The kind of inquiry that emerged in the nineteenth century to resolve these issues was, of course, what we now call 'educational research' – a form of non-theoretical, methodical inquiry, which, at least in principle, aspired to portray itself as an applied social science and which, in practice, accepted the prevailing utilitarian view of education and educational change. Thus, as education was itself transformed from a morally informed species of *praxis* into a state-controlled system of schooling, so educational inquiry was transformed from a form of inquiry in which questions about the role of education in creating the good society could be adequately expressed, into a form of research that was constrained by the liberal and utilitarian assumptions on which the state system of schooling had been erected and confined to the version of the good society that the state officially endorsed.

Any full-length version of this history of educational research would have to show how, in the mid-twentieth century, the assumption that educational inquiry belonged to the classical tradition of practical philosophy was subjected to a prolonged barrage of heavy-handed criticisms by modern analytic and scientifically minded philosophers and replaced by a somewhat arbitrary collection of academic disciplines – the philosophy, psychology, sociology and history 'of education' (Tibble 1966; Peters 1973). In particular, it would need to show how the kind of 'philosophy of education' that emerged in the 1960s was, in part, the result of a desire to purge practical philosophy of its concern with the role of education in creating the good society and replace it with an academically respectable and value-neutral form of 'theoretical' philosophy that would be uncontaminated by value-laden political concerns (O'Connor 1957; Peters 1966).

What this history of educational inquiry may also wish to consider is the place to be accorded to those isolated attempts that have been made by some recent social philosophers and educational theorists to create a renewed awareness of the contemporary significance of practical philosophy for the human sciences in general (Gadamer 1967, 1980; Flyvbjerg 2001) and educational research in particular (Schwab 1969; Elliott 1987; Carr 1995). What, finally, it may wish to reveal is the extent to which the Marxist approach to the sociology of education that emerged in the 1970s under the general name of 'reproduction theory' (Bowles and Gintis 1976; Apple 1982; Hartnett and Naish 1990) was based on nothing other than a reiteration of an insight as old as Plato: that education cannot be investigated as something 'external' to society and always has to be understood as an intrinsic and dynamic part of the general process of social evolution – the process through which the cultural, political and economic life of a society is simultaneously reproduced and transformed.

Conclusion

My efforts to sketch the broad contours of these two histories of educational research obviously leave a lot to be desired. However, I hope that they are sufficient to make clear how the first of these histories not only provides the starting point for our present understanding of educational research. It also constitutes the end point of a second much longer and larger historical narrative about how an earlier form of educational inquiry has, in our own modern times, been largely abandoned and disowned. Of course, from the perspective provided by my first history – a history that reads the past in terms of the present – the idea that educational research is a species of practical philosophy will be dismissed as outmoded and methodologically naive, an idea that simply reflects the intellectually impoverished pre-modern times in which it was our predecessors' misfortune to live. Indeed, from this historical perspective, any form of educational inquiry that pre-dates its modern nineteenth-century formation will be dismissed as pre-history: as having little more than antiquarian interest with nothing to contribute to our current concerns.

However, once we begin to consider the present condition of educational research from my second historical perspective, some interesting insights begin to emerge. What first begins to emerge is some understanding of how the modern transformation of education into schooling has so removed education from the sphere of *praxis* as to virtually eliminate ethical categories from the legitimate field of educational enquiry and research. Technologization and institutionalization – those very central pillars of the culture of modernity – effectively ensure that education is now understood as synonymous with state schooling and hence as an activity conducted for utilitarian and economic purposes, rather than as an ethical activity directed towards morally desirable or socially transformative ends. As a result, the notion of educational inquiry as a species of practical philosophy has become obsolete and educational research has been reduced to a mundane technical expertise in which non-technical, non-expert questions about the role of education in creating the good society are no longer asked. Deprived of both cultural resources and intellectual expression, it is hardly surprising that our understanding of educational research as a form of practical philosophy has all but disappeared.

What also emerges is some explanation of the perceived 'irrelevance' of so much contemporary educational research. For what in its modern formation educational research supplies is a collection of isolated and often contradictory 'findings' that, because they can find no place in any unified or integrated theoretical whole, are quite incapable of making any coherent response to fundamental questions about what the role of education in modern society should be. Thus the depoliticization of education that resulted from the reduction of education to schooling, and the fragmentation of educational research into a series of disconnected and irrelevant findings, are not unrelated events. Rather, the depoliticization of education was itself aided and assisted by the replacement of a version of educational inquiry in which fundamental political questions about the purpose of education in creating the good society were accorded formal recognition, with a form of educational research in which these questions were no longer regarded as being of significant concern.

The third and final conclusion to emerge is that a necessary prerequisite to any serious attempt to examine the present critical state of educational research is the introduction of new ways of interpreting its past. One of the key requirements of any such interpretation is that it should recognize that there can be no timeless ahistorical understanding of educational research 'as such'. Another is that it does not remain blind to the possibility that our current understanding of educational research would not – and perhaps could not – have taken its contemporary methodical form unless our long-standing understanding of educational inquiry as part of the tradition of practical philosophy had not already been transformed. The history of this transformation has yet to be written. But it is only by virtue of such a history that we will ensure that we will no longer continue to conflate education inquiry with that particular understanding of its meaning that the nineteenth-century system of state schooling has bequeathed.

References

Abrams, P. (1968) *The Origins of British Sociology 1834–1914*. Chicago, IL: University of Chicago Press.

Apple, M.W. (ed.) (1982) *Cultural and Economic Reproduction in Education*. London: Routledge & Kegan Paul.

Bain, A. (1879) *Education as Science*. London: Kegan Paul.

Booth, C. (1902) *The Life and Labour of the People of London*. London: Macmillan.

Bowles, S. and Gintis, H. (1976) *Schooling in Capitalist America: Education Reform and the Contradictions of Economic Life*. London: Routledge & Kegan Paul.

Carr, W. (1995) *For Education: Towards Critical Educational Inquiry*. Buckingham: Open University Press.

Elliott, J. (1987) Educational theory, practical philosophy and action research, *British Journal of Educational Studies*, 25(2): 149–69.

Feinberg, W. (1983) *Understanding Education*. Cambridge: Cambridge University Press.

Flyvbjerg, B. (2001) *Making Social Science Matter – Why Social Inquiry Fails and How it can Succeed Again*. Cambridge: Cambridge University Press.

Gadamer, H.G. (1967) Theory, technology, practice: the task of the science of man, *Social Research*, 44: 529–61.

Gadamer, H.G. (1980) Practical philosophy as a model of the human sciences, *Research in Phenomenology*, 9: 74–85.

Hamilton, D. (1990) *Learning about Education*. Buckingham: Open University Press.

Hartnett, A. and Naish, M. (1990) Schooling and society, in N. Entwistle (ed.) *Handbook of Educational Ideas and Practices*. London: Routledge.

O'Connor, D.J. (1957) *An Introduction to the Philosophy of Education*. London: Routledge & Kegan Paul.

Peters, R.S. (1966) *Ethics and Education*. London: Allen & Unwin.

Peter, R.S. (1973) Education as an academic discipline, *British Journal of Educational Studies*, 21: 2.

Simon, J. (1970) *The Social Origins of English Education*. London: Routledge.

Tibble, J.W. (ed.) (1966) *The Study of Education*. London: Routledge & Kegan Paul.

Schwab, J.J. (1969) The practical: a language for curriculum, *School Review*, 78: 1–24.

2 | Towards a social history of educational research

Gary McCulloch

A theme that educational researchers have tended to neglect, certainly in Britain, is the history of educational research itself. This chapter seeks to encourage further research in this area. It does so from a standpoint that such history should not only be intrinsically interesting and rewarding in its own right, but also provide explanatory leverage on the problems and dilemmas of our own time. More than this, indeed, it can help to challenge the assumptions and values that are incorporated in contemporary educational discourse. As the late Brian Simon (1966) trenchantly observed, 'There is, perhaps, no more liberating influence than the knowledge that things have not always been as they are and need not remain so' (p. 92). One such set of values, frequently referred to by the contributors to this volume, is the supposed dichotomy between 'rigour' and 'relevance' in current parlance. A historical understanding of educational research helps us to reconstruct the debate around these terms and to approach them in different ways, as well as allowing us to trace the origins of the contemporary debate.

The case for social history

There are at least two important reasons why the history of educational research deserves greater attention than it has hitherto received. The first of these is that it can provide a means of understanding the contemporary crisis of educational research, and the solutions that have been developed for addressing this crisis. Over the past decade, educational research has come under intense public criticism from a range of well-placed and influential sources. In his Teacher Training Agency lecture of 1996, for example, David Hargreaves sparked fierce controversy over his claims that a radical change was required 'both in the kind of research that is done and the way in which it is organised' (Hargreaves 1996: 1). According to Hargreaves, the public money spent on educational research was 'poor value for money in terms of improving the quality of education provided in schools' (p. 1). Educational research, he claimed, was largely 'non-cumulative', partly because 'few researchers seek to create a body of knowledge which is then tested, extended or replaced in some systematic way' (p. 2). Indeed, Hargreaves asserted, 'Given the huge amounts of educational research conducted over the last fifty years or more, there are few areas which have yielded a corpus of research evidence regarded as scientifically sound and as worthwhile research to guide professional action – and this is true in areas which might be regarded as fundamental' (p. 2). Educational research was in his view caught between two stools, on the one hand 'the basic social sciences (psychology, sociology)', and on the other 'practitioners in schools', and tended to receive recognition from neither camp. Hargreaves concluded that there was an urgent need to end 'the frankly second-rate educational research which does not make a serious contribution to fundamental theory or knowledge; which is irrelevant to practice; which is uncoordinated with any preceding or follow-up research; and which clutters up academic journals that virtually nobody reads' (p. 7).

There are several key claims and assertions in Hargreaves' critique that demand not only philosophical analysis such as has already been provided, for example, by Hammersley (1997), but also historical investigation. The notion of educational research as a form of science in which researchers 'seek to create a body of knowledge which is then tested, extended or replaced in some systematic way' is one such issue. The idea of educational research as an investment intended directly to improve the quality of education provided in schools is another. The images of 'rigour' and 'relevance' evoked in Hargreaves' account provide yet a third. Rigour is equated with the social sciences, fundamental theory and knowledge; relevance is associated with the demands of classroom practitioners in schools and with improved educational outcomes. How far does a history of educational research either justify or challenge such claims? In what ways does it reflect a basic continuity with the past, or else a fundamental shift in purposes and interests? And to what extent does it question these assumptions and the dichotomies that they generate by illuminating possible alternatives and differences in approaching the problems of educational research? Addressing these issues is an important means of evaluating and problematizing Hargreaves' criticisms, and potentially of reconstructing the debate that has followed. Yet little has been done to attempt to explore them in any deep or detailed way, still less to use them either to explain the difficulties identified by Hargreaves or to articulate alternative approaches.

The initiatives that have developed since Hargreaves' 1996 lecture have overwhelmingly colluded in expressing similar basic assumptions about the nature and problems of educational research. The Tooley Report of 1998 concerned itself with the 'quality' of educational research (Tooley 1998), the

Hillage Report of the same year with its dissemination (Hillage *et al.* 1998), the Economic and Social Research Council's Teaching and Learning Research Programme with measurable improvements to learning outcomes, and the National Educational Research Forum (NERF) with the cumulative and systematic review of research findings. None of these entered into a discussion about the historical origins or basis of the problems that they identified, or of the solutions that they propose [see, for example, Ball (2001) on NERF's proposals]. Perhaps more surprisingly, scholarly commentaries on these initiatives have also so far shed little light on the historical implications of these developments. For example, Elliott and Doherty (2001), in their otherwise helpful discussion of the 'neo-liberal' and 'Third Way' aspects of the Labour government's approach to educational research, fail to develop any meaningful historical purchase on the issues they examine.

The second reason why the history of educational research should itself be the subject of research is that it will help to inform the further development of a community or profession of educational researchers. A community such as this requires an awareness of its own history for it to define its goals and purposes for the future. It needs to be able to assess the extent and nature of its past successes to appraise how to build on them; it needs to understand its past failures to learn from them. It needs an archive of precedents to guide suggested changes; it needs an active memory to draw on earlier events to make sense of current ones. Individual educational researchers each have their own store of personal memories to give them a basis for their further development; in some cases, this stretches back decades. To foster a professional memory for an entire community entails converting these personal and private resources into the public arena, providing some basis for sharing and debating them, and ensuring that they are not lost when individuals retire or die. It also means developing a mode of reflexivity, becoming self-critical and aware of its own limitations in the light of experience, and responding to contemporary changes and challenges by re-evaluating the lessons of its past, which are commonly ascribed as traditions (on distinctions between 'private' and 'public' pasts in education, see McCulloch 1997, 2000).

The most suitable kind of approach to the history of educational research is as a form of social history. That is, it should highlight the connections between the historical development of educational research and broader social, cultural and political issues. If approached in these terms, the history of educational research will not simply be a history of ideas, and will not be understood in isolation from broader contexts and structures. It will be critical of the underlying assumptions of educational research. It will also be alert to issues of power and status, to sites of conflict over the nature of educational research, and to the micropolitics of institutions engaged in it. If it is concerned with the structures of such research, it will be no less committed to understanding the researchers themselves.

The idea of a social history of educational research may be contrasted in some respects with the short history of the area recently essayed by Verma and Mallick (1999: ch. 4). This is a rather bland and uncritical treatment that emphasizes the importance of the development of psychometric measurement, but does very little to indicate the shortcomings or failures of such work. It also fails to challenge the assumptions underlying current discourses, suggesting, for example, that since working relations between educational policy makers have tended to break down, 'the idea that research is an individually defined project conducted by the individual may have to become, largely, a thing of the past' (Verma and Mallick 1999: 69). According to Verma and Mallick (1999: 70):

> This will not entirely prevent individuals from pursuing their own interests – charitable trusts will continue to fund research that can be supported by their trustees. The main body of work, however, will be defined, effectively, by the government, since that is the source of most of the funding and most researchers will be engaged in it.

Such accounts fail to problematize the social, cultural and political implications of this kind of development either in the past or in the present.

To be fair, there is already some work that has started to sketch out a social history approach in this area. In this country, Janet Finch's (1986) book, *Research and Policy*, is highly instructive as an example of what may be possible. Finch discussed how quantitative approaches to research have historically been dominant in social and educational policy-oriented studies, while qualitative approaches have constituted a weaker alternative tradition. Although qualitative methods have been seen as 'soft, subjective and speculative', according to Finch, quantitative methods were regarded as 'hard, objective and rigorous' (p. 5). She suggests that the key formative phase in developing these relationships was the early Victorian period of the 1830s and 1840s, strongly influenced by the prevailing need at that time for administrative intelligence and an intellectual climate that favoured positivism (p. 113). The dominant approach to social research and social policy henceforward, according to Finch, involved:

> the impartial collection of facts; an unproblematic conception of 'facts', based on a positivist epistemology; a belief in the direct utility of such facts in shaping measures of social reform which can be implemented by governments; and a strong preference for statistical methods and the social survey as the most suitable technique for fact-collecting.
>
> (Finch 1986: 37)

As a result of this prevailing approach, Finch suggests, there has been little scope for qualitative work, which has had very little place in government reports.

The alternative British tradition of qualitative research Finch finds, for example, in the Mass Observation movement of the 1930s and 1940s, which drew on the model of anthropology. According to Finch, such initiatives differed from the dominant quantitative approach, in that

> the approach to data-creation goes beyond concepts of unproblematic fact-gathering; there is a more explicit recognition of the process of undertaking research as a political activity in the broadest sense, and the knowledge thereby created as intrinsically political; and there is an approach to policy-related research which reflects the view from below, not the view from above.
>
> (Finch 1986: 94)

Finch goes on to propose that this under-utilized alternative tradition to research should be drawn on much more fully in social and educational policies in the future.

Finch's study is highly significant as an approach that should illuminate the history of educational research. It is notable, nevertheless, that Finch is not herself principally an educational researcher, but rather draws mainly on educational examples to make a more general case about the nature of social policy research in Britain. There still remains a major need and opportunity to examine the case of educational research in much more detail. In the United States, a major contribution towards a more specific social history of educational research has recently been produced by Ellen Condliffe Lagemann. Lagemann (2000) explores how the idea of education as a 'science' influenced the nature of educational research and tended 'to push the field in unfortunate directions – away from close interactions with policy and practice and toward excessive quantification and scientism' (p. xi). She emphasizes that the history of educational scholarship is not 'the isolated history of an intellectual field', but should be regarded as 'an ongoing story about larger constellations of social values and views that have often found their clearest manifestations in debates about education, including education research' (p. xiii). Disciplines themselves, as she avers, 'are socially constructed and change over time; they are made, not given in nature'. Therefore, according to Lagemann,

> By problematizing definitions of academic and professional fields, discipline history seeks to reconstruct the processes by which maps of knowledge are created. By emphasizing that currently taken-for-granted intellectual constructs did not necessarily exist in their familiar forms in earlier eras, it calls attention to conflicts and negotiations as well as to patterns of historical choice and chance.
>
> (Lagemann 2000: xiv)

With this in mind, she approaches the topic in terms of 'the changing ecology of knowledge and the politics that has been part of that' (p. xiv; see also Lagemann 1997).

Lagemann appraises the historical development of educational research as a 'contested terrain', but one that has been dominated principally by the idea of an empirical and professional science, based mainly on behaviourist psychology and quantitative measurement. Other approaches, including that developed by John Dewey at the University of Chicago, tended to be marginalized, although they were never entirely overcome. Lagemann goes on to argue that educational research became isolated from other areas of study in universities and also from practitioners in schools largely because of the 'narrow problematics' that characterized the field from an early stage (Lagemann 2000: 235). The technical and individualistic character of educational research was well established by about 1920: 'It was more narrowly instrumental than genuinely investigatory in an open-ended, playful way . . . Useable knowledge, quite narrowly defined, had become the *sine qua non* of educational study' (p. 236). Moreover, according to Lagemann, educational psychology, at the core of educational research, was both narrowly behaviourist in its outlook and individualistic rather than social: 'It simply ignored the degree to which multiple factors, including subtle interactions between and among individuals, groups, cultural traditions, and social structures, all combine to influence teaching and learning' (Lagemann 2000: 236).

Thus, Lagemann's historical account of educational research in the United States presents an explanation for the problems of the field, and also informs and challenges current assumptions about how to proceed towards the future. As she concludes,

> Viewed as an accurate, yet purposive reconstruction, history can perhaps become an instrument of reform. Those elements in the history of educational scholarship that are troubling – everything from the attitudes revealed about education to the penchant shown for translating complex ideas into formulaic principles – may thus become guides to change.
>
> (Lagemann 2000: 246)

The issue for educational research in Britain is how to develop the kind of social history that will perform a similar role.

Educational studies or educational research?

One way of pursuing the social history of educational research in Britain is to investigate earlier ideas about 'rigour' and 'relevance'. This may help us to trace the origins of the current orthodoxies that have been popularized by Hargreaves and others, and also highlight alternative modes of understanding these terms. A promising framework for addressing these issues is to examine the tensions that have developed between two distinctly different and opposing viewpoints in research about education: 'educational studies' and 'educational research'. The latter approaches education as a single and autonomous discipline, a hard, empirical and scientific endeavour. This appears to represent the dominant approach to research in education in Britain, rooted in the rise of educational psychology in the early decades of the twentieth century and consolidated over the past thirty years.

By contrast, adherents of educational studies have favoured a pluralist and eclectic approach, seeking to apply a range of disciplines from the social sciences and humanities, rather than seeing education as a single or unitary discipline in itself. A grounding in the disciplines or in one particular discipline is seen as essential as a means of understanding educational theories and practices. The key disciplines in this respect have generally been regarded to be history, philosophy, sociology and psychology, although others such as economics have also been emphasized at different times. In one sense, the disciplines were established separately, as distinct and discrete disciplinary communities, each with their own endeavours and priorities, and each with their own bases in research and teaching. They all involved specialization in a particular mode of analysis, demanded a specific form of expertise and claimed their own unique inheritance of a tradition of knowledge and values. Equally, they were dedicated to following the intellectual currents of their 'parent' disciplines practised broadly across the university, often to the extent of being subordinated by them. In another sense, the disciplines were established separately, as complementary approaches to the study of education. It was the combination of their different forms of expertise that was taken to be the most effective means of addressing the problems and processes of education. The disciplines, therefore, signalled a pluralist vision of educational studies that sought to draw on a wide range of human knowledge and experience. The problems of education are approached in relation to broader social, cultural, political and historical issues, of which they are perceived to be a part (for a discussion of the history of educational studies on which this section draws, see McCulloch 2002).

This kind of approach to the problems of education has also informed particular notions of rigour and relevance. From this perspective, rigour is derived from disciplinary study, as opposed to conceiving education as a separate or isolated endeavour. A classic expression of this view was that of Richard Peters. In his inaugural lecture as professor of the philosophy of education at the Institute of Education, London, in 1963, Peters insisted that 'education is not an autonomous discipline, but a field, like politics, where the disciplines of history, philosophy, psychology, and sociology have application' (Peters 1980: 273). This conviction reflected a conscious reaction against what Peters described as the 'undifferentiated mush' of educational theory, which, in his view, had 'contributed so much to the low standing of the study of education in this country'. At the same time, relevance was understood in terms of the integration of educational issues with the more general social and political problems of the day; that is, the study of education was held to have a broad relevance to public concerns.

The heyday of educational studies was in the period from the 1940s until the 1970s. It rose to prominence in the years following the Second World War and the Education Act of 1944, as part of a concerted attempt both to reform education and improve society. It came under increasing challenge from the 1970s onwards, especially after the so-called 'Great Debate' on education launched in 1976 by the Labour prime minister James Callaghan, and Conservative policies after 1979 which encouraged very different ideas about rigour and relevance. The *British Journal of Educational Studies*, established in 1952, reflected the concerns of the educational studies movement. On the one hand, it strove not to be 'narrowly specialist', but rather to 'serve the needs and interests of everyone concerned with education whom the implications of specialised research affect'. Its 'broad objects' were defined as being 'to explain the significance of new thought, to provide philosophical discussion at a high level, and to deepen existing interest in the purposes and problems of current educational policy' (*BJES* 1952: 67). On the other hand, it offered specialized study rooted in the separate disciplines. It was within these terms of reference that the journal sought to define and explore the implications of 'rigour' and 'relevance' in relation to education.

The challenge of establishing disciplines that would be both distinctive in their approaches yet also interdependent in their contributions to educational studies yielded fruit in the 1960s and early 1970s in several tangible ways. Their interdependence was fostered in a number of published works intended for students of education, and also in the rise of the new area of curriculum studies. At the same time, stimulated by a rapid expansion in initial teacher education and the teaching opportunities that this presented, separate and distinct disciplinary communities became consolidated. This process was marked by the creation of new journals, conferences and associations that were devoted to the promotion of teaching and research in these specific domains.

Probably the best known published work of the period to promote a disciplinary approach to educational studies was *The Study of Education*, edited by J.W. Tibble (1966) of the University of Leicester. It was produced as an introduction to an ambitious venture entitled the 'Students Library of Education', published by Routledge and Kegan Paul. Tibble's edited collection was intended to explore the nature of education as a subject of study, and the nature of its contributory disciplines. The contributors to the collection were Paul Hirst of King's College, London, on educational theory, Richard Peters of the Institute of Education, London, on the philosophy of education, Brian Simon of the University of Leicester on the history of education, Ben Morris of the University of Bristol on the role of psychology, and William Taylor, also of the University of Bristol, on the sociology of education. Again the notion of rigour was articulated with reference to the application of the disciplines to educational problems, most explicitly in the case of Hirst's essay, in which he insisted:

> It is only by rigorous work within these forms, according to their own critical canons, that valid reasons can be brought to the formation of educational principles. If work or study in the theory is to be anything but superficial it must readily become differentiated out into the serious and systematic treatment of the relevant philosophical, sociological or historical questions that are raised.
>
> (Hirst 1966: 55)

The Students Library of Education was itself an imposing monument to disciplinary studies. It was intended that the Library should consist of a series of basic books, each of 25,000 to 30,000 words in length, and available for students in paperback editions. As Tibble noted, some would illustrate the separate contributions of the different disciplines to the study of education, while others would deal with a major educational topic in an interdisciplinary way, 'showing the contributions which different forms of thought can make to it' (Tibble 1966: vii).

This dominant set of assumptions was strengthened further in the late 1960s and early 1970s through the rise of 'curriculum studies' as an approach to educational studies. This area was stimulated by the development of curriculum initiatives and, in particular, the activities of the Schools Council for the Curriculum and Examinations, established in 1964, which were expected to transform the character of the school curriculum. Curriculum studies, designed to evaluate the success of these new initiatives and to understand them in their broader context, was deeply imbued with a disciplinary outlook, reflected, for example, in the ideas of John F. Kerr, professor of education at the University of Leicester. In his inaugural lecture, 'The problem of curriculum reform', presented in January 1967, Kerr sought to encourage broader attention to issues of curriculum change. He was confident as to the prospects of the new curriculum initiatives, but was concerned that those involved in such initiatives were basing their decisions principally upon experience and personal judgements. He called, therefore, for more research and evaluation to build into the process a more coherent theoretical framework. Kerr argued that philosophy, psychology, sociology and history, in cooperation with each other, could make a major contribution towards this end. He also proposed that practising educationists should be able to consult specialists in the disciplines for advice about particular problems 'in the same way as the medical profession calls upon physiologists, biochemists, bacteriologists and so on' (Kerr 1968: 36). This acknowledgement of the needs of teachers and practitioners marked a shift in emphasis in the idea of relevance, reflected also, for example, in the work of Denis Lawton at the Institute of Education during the 1970s (Lawton 1980).

Lawrence Stenhouse, director of the Schools Council Humanities Curriculum Project and then of the Centre for Applied Research in Education (CARE) at the University of East Anglia, similarly championed a disciplinary approach but was also concerned to make clear the potential relevance of educational studies to the needs of teachers. According to Stenhouse, the teaching of education as an undifferentiated field had been 'largely supplanted' by the teaching of constituent disciplines, especially in his view, philosophy, psychology and sociology. This change, he argued, had increased the 'rigour' and the 'intellectual tone' of education courses, but had done little for 'their relevance to the problem of improving the practice of teaching'. He proposed the further development of curriculum studies as a means of building on the disciplines to foster a close study of curriculum and teaching that would be relevant to practice in the schools (Stenhouse 1975: vii).

Nevertheless, while the disciplines continued to establish their complementary claims in relation to the general study of education, they also entrenched their separate disciplinary identities. This was reflected in particular in the philosophy of education and in the history of education in terms of collegial activities that led to the formation of new journals and societies in these areas. In 1965, the philosophy of education consolidated an avowedly analytical approach, derived especially from the so-called 'London School' led by Hirst and Peters, through the creation of the Philosophy of Education Society of Great Britain. This soon generated its own published proceedings, which, in turn, became the *Journal of Philosophy of Education*. Meanwhile, the history of education was represented formally through the establishment of the History of Education Society in 1967, leading again to regular newsletters and conferences as distinguishing marks of the disciplinary community.

A new journal, the *Journal of Educational Administration and History*, was formed in 1968, based at the University of Leeds. The new society established its own journal, entitled *History of Education*, in 1972. In common with philosophers of education, historians of education tended in the main to style themselves according to current trends in their parent discipline. It was notable, for example, that the leading social historian, Asa Briggs, was invited to contribute the first article in *History of Education*, and the paramount intention was clear from his very first sentence, which ran: 'The study of the history of education is best considered as part of the wider study of the history of the history of society, social history with the politics, economics and, it is necessary to add, the religion put in' (Briggs 1972: 160). This outlook encouraged an emphasis on disciplinary rigour and relevance to the broader concerns of society, but also a somewhat reckless disregard of specifically educational problems that increasingly exposed historians of education in education departments to a charge of irrelevance.

From the Great Debate onwards, education came under increasing scrutiny to be more accountable to current social and economic demands, leading to a growing emphasis on 'practical' approaches at the expense of 'theory'. This general trend was reflected both in courses in education – for teacher training and continuing professional development – and in research. At the same time, 'educational research' was increasingly advanced as a unitary and autonomous kind of study in its own right. In 1974, the British Educational Research Association (BERA) was founded as a major initiative to unite educationists around a common cause and a single organization. Its flagship journal, the *British Educational Research Journal*, founded in the same year, pursued the goal of forging a single body of knowledge from the disparate traditions that had hitherto held sway. By the 1990s, Michael Bassey, executive secretary of BERA, sought to make a rigid distinction between 'educational research' and disciplinary research conducted in educational settings. Research in educational settings, according to Bassey (1995), is only 'educational research' if it is 'concerned with attempts to improve educational judgements and actions' (p. 37). Indeed, he argued,

> It is particularly important that educational research be recognised as research that aims critically to inform educational judgements and decisions in order to improve educational action, while sociological, psychological, historical and philosophical research in education are concerned critically to inform understandings of discipline-pertinent phenomena in educational settings.
>
> (Bassey 1995: 39)

On this view, a dependence on the disciplines could be seen not only as unduly theoretical and tenuous in its connections with educational concerns, but as restrictive in holding back the growth of an independent field of inquiry. Not far from the surface, too, is a progressive, scientific, ahistorical model of research that is systematically detached from the moorings of disciplinary endeavours. It finds frequent echo in the arguments of other recent critics who argue that educational research should be defined principally in terms of its usefulness, or in relation to its tangible influence on specific learning outcomes.

There has, therefore, been an underlying historical tension between 'educational studies' on the one hand and 'educational research' on the other. Exponents of educational studies have stimulated a pluralist approach to the study of education, one that has drawn opportunistically from the humanities and social sciences to seek to understand and address the changing problems of education. They have formed a loose coalition of disparate factions, as opposed to a single homogeneous group. In many cases, discipline-based studies were aligned more clearly to the parent discipline than to the study of education, and they could often be remote from educational practice. A core disciplinary audience tended to be given precedence over a general educational audience that was seeking applications to general problems. Against this, links between theory and practice did not go entirely unremarked. Interesting and significant attempts were made to establish useful connections between them, especially through combining the insights of the disciplines, for example in curriculum studies and the Students Library of Education. They also valued rigour and relevance, but attached very different meanings to these ideals to those that were to become commonplace by the end of the century.

Conclusions

The historical tensions that are sketched out in the case of 'educational studies' and 'educational research' provide some clues to the kind of work that is required to develop a social history of educational research. To pursue it in greater depth, it will be necessary to engage in detailed study of the institutions involved. Such agencies include the associations and societies that have been established to defend and promote particular approaches, such as the various disciplinary societies and also BERA itself. They also include the journals that have developed to represent and disseminate educational research, like the *British Journal of Educational Psychology*, the *British Journal of Educational Studies* and the *British Educational Research Journal*. Conferences in educational research, like the Standing Conference on Studies in Education that developed from the 1950s, and the Westhill Sociology of Education conference in the 1980s, should also be examined closely. These should be regarded as sites that have often been contested between rival values and interests. A similar approach may be taken to the agencies that have sought to mediate the encroaching interests of the State with those of researchers in education, such as the Schools Council in the 1960s and 1970s and NERF in the early years of the twenty-first century. Reports such as the Tooley and Hillage reports of 1998 should also be located in their historical contexts. The historical development of individual institutions, such as university education departments and teacher training colleges, is also suitable for this kind of study. At the same time, it would be useful to develop detailed investigations of the role of key figures in the field, such as Lawrence Stenhouse, Basil Bernstein and Brian Simon, and of leading educational administrators, like Derek Morrell and Anthony Part. It is also important to recapture the voices of the broad mass of educational researchers, which should not be omitted from the historical account. There are, indeed, many research projects that deserve to be initiated, both for their own sake and for their potential contribution to the broader project of a social history of educational research.

For the purposes of this broader project, it has been argued that such studies need to be alert to the broader social, cultural and political dimensions of educational research, and to the conflicts of values and interests that have so often been present in the discourse of research. They also need to comprehend the changes and continuities that have developed over time, including those that have influenced and shaped our contemporary orthodoxies. We are as yet only at the very early stages of such a project. If it can be pursued energetically over the next decade, the potential is there for it to make a powerful contribution to our understanding of our history and education and, in terms of educational research itself, to play a significant part in reconstructing the debate.

References

Ball, S. (2001) 'You've been NERFed!' Dumbing down the academy: National Educational Research Forum: 'a national strategy – consultation paper': a brief and bilious response, *Journal of Education Policy*, 16(3): 265–8.

Bassey, M. (1995) *Creating Education Through Research: A Global Perspective of Educational Research for the Twenty-First Century*. Newark: Kirkington Moor Press.

Briggs, A. (1972) The study of the history of education, *History of Education*, 1(1): 5–16.

Elliott, J. and Doherty, P. (2001) Restructuring educational research for the 'Third Way'?, in M. Fielding (ed.) *Taking Education Really Seriously: Four Years' Hard Labour*. London: Routledge Falmer.

Finch, J. (1986) *Research and Policy: The Uses of Qualitative Methods in Social and Educational Research*. London: Falmer Press.

Hammersley, M. (1997) Educational research and teaching: a response to David Hargreaves' TTA lecture, *British Educational Research Journal*, 23(2): 141–61.

Hargreaves, D. (1996) Teaching as a research-based profession: possibilities and prospects, Teacher Training Agency Annual Lecture, London, March.

Hillage, J., Pearson, R., Anderson, A. and Tamkin, P. (1998) *Excellence in Research on Schools*. London: Department for Education and Employment.

Hirst, P. (1966) Educational theory, in J.W. Tibble (ed.) *The Study of Education*. London: Routledge & Kegan Paul.

Kerr, J.F. (1968) The problem of curriculum reform, in J.F. Kerr (ed.) *Changing the Curriculum*. London: University of London Press.

Lagemann, E.C. (1997) Contested terrain: a history of education research in the United States, 1890–1990, *Educational Researcher*, 26(9): 5–17.

Lagemann, E.C. (2000) *An Elusive Science: The Troubling History of Education Research*. London: University of Chicago Press.

Lawton, D. ([1978] 1980) The end of the secret garden?, in P. Gordon (ed.) *The Study of Education*, Vol. 2. London: Woburn.

McCulloch, G. (1997) Privatising the past? History and education policy in the 1990s, *British Journal of Educational Studies*, 45(1): 69–82.

McCulloch, G. (2000) Publicising the educational past, in D. Crook and R. Aldrich (eds) *History of Education for the 21st Century*. London: Institute of Education.

McCulloch, G. (2002) 'Disciplines contributing to education'? Educational studies and the disciplines, *British Journal of Educational Studies*, 50(1): 100–19.

Peters, R. ([1963] 1980) Education as initiation, in P. Gordon (ed.) *The Study of Education*, Vol. 1. London: Woburn.

Simon, B. (1966) The history of education, in J.W. Tibble (ed.) *The Study of Education*. London: Routledge & Kegan Paul.

Stenhouse, L. (1975) *An Introduction to Curriculum Research and Development*. London: Heinemann.

Tibble, J.W. (ed.) (1966) *The Study of Education*. London: Routledge & Kegan Paul.

Tooley, J. with Darby, D. (1998) *Educational Research: A Critique*. London: Office for Standards in Education.

Verma, G. and Mallick, K. (1999) *Researching Education: Perspectives and Techniques*. London: Falmer Press.

3 | Living research: thoughts on educational research as moral practice

Pat Sikes and Ivor Goodson

Introduction

Picture the scene: it's late in the evening and you're in the bar at a conference with colleagues and friends, some of whom you've not seen for a while, and someone starts reminiscing. 'Do you remember . . .?' Often the stories are about particular characters, their idiosyncrasies, proclivities and by now legendary exploits. Sometimes though, the emphasis is on times past (*a la recherché de temps perdu*), on recalling a *zeitgeist*, shared beliefs and values, commitments and motivations, good times, hard times, with evaluations coloured by what it's like now and our relative fortunes in different areas of our lives. We may come away from such sessions with regret for what's lost, or in gratitude that it's different now. If our imaginary conference is educational, in England, and if the company includes people aged around 45 plus, who have liberal or radical values, the chances are that some of the conversations will, no doubt, be about the 1960s and 1970s, covering curriculum development and innovation, Lawrence Stenhouse, the Schools' Council, democratic education, Countesthorpe College, and on how committed young women and men became teachers because they passionately and personally believed that the fast route to social reform, to social justice, was through education and schooling.

For educational researchers, those days were heady ones because there was a lot of optimism around and the 'profession' was growing and flourishing. During this time, a social identity as an educational researcher became more widely available and it's likely that many of those joining in our conversation will have taken it on then, often with the moral aim of acting as 'public intellectuals' (Goodson 1997), assisting in the task of social reconstruction and working for democratic education.

With hindsight, and in the light of the election of the Thatcher government and the ascendancy of the 'New Right', such optimism now appears naive and ingenuous and, left at this conclusion, our conversation might seem purely nostalgic, focusing on the 'might have beens' of a social democratic politics that was wilfully extinguished. It is, however, possible to regard those reminiscences as an example of collective memory (see Halbwachs 1992) that serves to sustain and pass on important understandings, beliefs and values that, while at risk because of the threat they may pose to current regimes and dominant ideologies, nonetheless provide 'resources for hope' in a continuing project of moral purpose and social mission.

It is our view that a battle has been, and continues to be, fought over the memories of educational researchers, and that systematic attempts have been made, by governments – Labour as well as Conservative – to help us to forget the morality that lay behind the quest for democratic education by defining 'new' ways of researching and creating new social identities of what it means to be a researcher (cf. Ball 2001: 211). As Rosen (1998) put it, 'there is often a social struggle to gain ascendancy over our memories and those who feel the pull (*of different cultures, beliefs and values*) will experience the dilemmas and often the pain of this battle fought out within their social consciousness' (p. 131, emphasis added).

In this chapter, we want to capitalize on the potential of collective memory to keep alive and transmit values and beliefs as we explore notions of research as moral practice. Specifically, we will focus on our shared memories, approaching these from our personal autobiographies through life history.

In taking a life-history approach, our intention is to demonstrate the influence that life experiences can have upon the development of individual educational researchers' professional values and practice, thereby shaping the collective professional values and practice of educational research communities. We see life history as being particularly appropriate because it highlights our fundamental belief that moral research practice, whether at an individual, team, institutional or national level, is grounded in personal decisions and that personal decisions have to do with personal, subjective experiences and perceptions – located within, and influenced by, particular historical contexts (for our conceptualization of life history, see Goodson and Sikes 2001). We share Tierney's (2000) view that 'a goal of life history work in a post-modern age is to break the stranglehold of meta-narratives that establish rules of truth, legitimacy and identity' (p. 546). We hold, as have many others before us, that the personal is political, and that individual perceptions, decisions and experiences can come to have wider significance and implications for other people. Instances that speak to this for us are: Martin Niemöller's powerful piece, which recounts how, when the Nazis came for various groups of people – Jews, gypsies, trade unionists, homosexuals – he said nothing because he wasn't a member of those groups and how, when they finally came for him, there was no-one to speak on his behalf; Hannah Arendt's description of 'the banality of evil' as exemplified by Eichman, and her injunction for individuals to stop and think; Martin Luther King's dream; and Rosa Parks' decision to sit down on the bus.

Given our focus, these examples may seem to be overdrawn. However, educational research is often concerned with social justice issues and can, ultimately, have implications for life chances – the research of Cyril Burt, which provided the basis for the 11+ examination in England and Wales, is a clear example here. Therefore, the origins and subsequent development of individual educational researchers' notions regarding moral research practice can be seen to have far-reaching consequences that warrant 'big' comparisons.

Before moving on to offer our life histories, we want to ground them in the contexts of thoughts about:

- the researcher in the research process, researcher positionality;
- the moment, the *zeitgeist*, with regard to educational research;
- the use of life history to investigate social phenomena;
- moral practice in educational research.

The researcher in the research process

Research practice cannot be disembodied. It is impossible to take the researcher out of any type of research or of any stage of the research process. The person of the researcher is always there, whether they be cast as 'villain', contaminating research design, data collection, analysis and reporting; as 'hero', whose intimate and influential involvement is an essential and fundamental constituent of the research; or as something in-between. It seems to us that the physical existence and presence of the living, perceiving, experiencing person who is the researcher is a constant reminder of the falseness of the positivist/qualitative, objective/subjective research dichotomy. This is because, as people, as social beings, located in space, time, cultural milieu, researchers (like anyone else) have been influenced by the particular understandings about, and interpretations of, the world to which they have been exposed. As Kuhn (1962) argued, there is no way to distinguish between what is subjective and perceived and in people's heads, and what is out there in the world. This is the consequence of perception and of language and there is no getting away from it. Nor is there any getting away from the influence differential experiences have on beliefs, values and world views, including notions of what constitutes moral research practice. Given that the researcher as person is already there, we must not pretend that it is possible to forget their personhood, their histories and all that that entails. Reflexivity should be an inherent and ubiquitous part of the research endeavour (see Hertz 1997). We should challenge the dogma, with its historical roots 'in the dominant Enlightenment worldview' (Christians 2000: 134), that good practice, *moral* practice, is value-free, neutral and objective and uncontaminated by the presence, in any way, shape or form, of the researcher. Furthermore, and in pursuit of moral research practice, we should reject the tradition of hiding ourselves by using discourse, which attempts to neutralize, minimize, standardize, contain, control, distance or disengage our subjective or personal experiences (Fine *et al.* 2000: 108–9). These matters do not, however, mean that the educational researcher cannot have as a major objective the task of being, to use James Baldwin's felicitous phrase, a 'moral witness'; indeed, we shall want to advocate precisely this position.

The moment

Other contributions to this book rehearse contemporary criticisms of educational research and various responses to them. For our purposes, suffice it to say that the central burden of the critique lies on value and values and on a particular definition or understanding of 'value'. That is, of 'value' for money and the 'values' of researchers as reflected in their choice of foci, methodologies and methods. Of course, value and values will only be questioned from the standpoint of there being other – different – values, and understandings of what equals good value, but it sometimes seems as if this fundamental truism is either obscured or conveniently forgotten. This sort of amnesia is perhaps characteristic of those who claim or assume rightness/goodness and the moral high ground on the basis of having the greatest power, maybe because, as Tierney (2000) notes, 'they are unable to grasp histories of groups and individuals except as these are constructed (or not) by current ideological forces' (p. 545). We would argue that the power presently lies with 'the market' and that the market definition of 'value' is entirely and systematically divorced from morality and emptied of moral meaning. Richard Sennett (1999) has recently written about the effects of the market on our moral character and purposes, an effect he summarizes as 'the corrosion of character'.

To elaborate: many people have written about the ways in which the educational debate reflects dominant local and global political climates. The values underlying these climates privilege a particular view of education as an adjunct of the economy and as a marketable commodity. This perception puts the emphasis on economic efficiency and accountability. On this view, an instrumental approach employing generally applied and specific technical and mechanistic procedures is the way to achieve the desired outcomes. A common consequence of this is that research which apparently provides value-free, objective and quantifiable evidence that can inform practice directly is favoured and funded. Another consequence, which has been realized in the UK, is the requirement of funding agencies that the researchers they sponsor be trained according to specified curriculum and in a specified manner.

As anyone who has ever had to teach a syllabus knows, the need to cover certain areas that will be assessed means that there is little or no time or space to address other ones that won't. Similarly, certain questions are less likely to be asked when what they relate to does not fit, or have legitimate meaning, within a dominant ideology. It seems to us that, frequently, the officially promulgated and endorsed agenda and associated discourse framing the focus, content and methodology of educational research does not allow for (some would say, systematically obscures) difficult questions about human difference, emotions and subjective perceptions. This, to our minds, is potentially demoralizing, in that it fails to acknowledge and, indeed, denies the essential uniqueness and individuality, the moral nature, of each human being – be they members of the research population or researchers. To put it bluntly, we are suggesting that the current trend or fashion (see Flyvbjerg 2001: 30) that emphasizes procedures and technical skills about both the practice of educational research and the induction of new researchers, may result in the systematic sidelining of moral concerns. The focus on delivery, in other words, obscures the question of distribution. We have, in effect, a concern with efficiency without any concern with equity. Practice is 'evidence-based', but the evidence is circumscribed. A national curriculum provides a recipe for social inclusion, while deriving from a curriculum that systematically encourages exclusion. To make such a system run 'effectively' is merely to make social exclusion more efficient. A rhetoric of standards, effective schools, accountability and inspection, all, therefore, mask the 'essential lie' that is the continuity of social reproduction and 'fine-tuning' of social stratification.

Life history

We have written at length both about the value of autobiographical and life-history approaches for studying educational topics, and about associated methodological moral and ethical issues (see, for example, Measor and Sikes 1992; Goodson 1995a; Sikes *et al.* 1996; Sikes 1997; Goodson and Sikes 2001). Here, our focus is on autobiographical life history: by that we mean our own stories set within the historical contexts relating to educational research in which we have lived them (see Goodson 1992: 6).

As we are using the approach, autobiographical life history implicitly and explicitly entails a moral commitment to honesty in that it requires – although cannot guarantee – that the subjects (i.e. ourselves) personally own beliefs and values. This involves acknowledging the influence of social positioning and differences, and issues of power of all kinds, including the 'power' to have one's work disseminated via conferences, journals, books, teaching, and so on.

Not least because of the possibilities it offers for self-publicity, academic autobiographical work has been criticized as 'self-indulgent' (see Mykhalovskiy 1997) 'vanity ethnography' (Maynard 1993: 329). Undoubtedly it can be that. Our reasons for choosing the approach are, however:

- to illustrate our journeys through the relatively recent, local history of educational research to serve as an example of how contexts can influence identities and notions of what it means to be a researcher and, more specifically, personal understandings of what constitutes 'moral' research [in doing this, we are making identity claims, justifying our conduct and beliefs, which, as MacLure (1993: 287) reminds us, is a moral enterprise in itself];
- because we believe that reflecting on our experiences and perceptions, owning them is a form of 'moral work and ethical practice' (Ellis and Bochner 2000: 747); and
- because, in showing how two careers are interrelated within an educational research community, even though, separated by generation (age), gender, institutional and geographical location, and occupational status, we are demonstrating the power of collective memory to transmit moral values and a shared sense of purpose.

Moral practice in educational research

Alasdair MacIntyre (1989) argues that the phrase 'moral practice' is tautologous, in that practice has to be either good or evil (and *for* good or evil). These words – 'good' and 'evil' – come, we would suggest, from a discourse that is not much used these days. Post-modern, poly-vocal, multi-perspective sensitivities can mean that making any value judgements is a fraught enterprise. (Or is this an example of the cowardice of the age?) If we talk about 'moral' research practice, then we are, at the least, implying that some practice is 'immoral'; and who are we to make such judgements?

Immoral, let alone evil, practice in educational research may seem, on the surface, a bit unlikely. We'd like to believe that everyone who is engaged in educational research starts from the position of wanting to make the world a better place in some way (following the Aristotelian ethical tradition; see MacIntyre 1981). This is a moral commitment to improvement of some kind, whether that be primarily in terms of adding to the sum of knowledge or, more immediately, by impacting on students' or teachers' experiences in some way to make them better (although there may be occasions when it is seen as justifiable to disadvantage some to benefit the common good). Of course, understandings of what equals better can vary depending on the value positions and notions of community that different individuals and groups subscribe to.

Richard Pring (2000) distinguishes between moral 'considerations which relate to general "principles of action" and those which relate to the dispositions and character of the researcher' (p. 141). With regard to the former: nowadays, adherence to an ethical code is usually invoked as evidence that subjects are safeguarded and that, therefore, research practice is moral. However, blanket codes, concerned with 'principles of action', can be seen to proceduralize and depersonalize and even, as Fine *et al.* (2000) point out, with specific reference to obtaining informed consent, may be seen as having the effect of absolving researchers of their moral responsibility:

> The consent form sits at the base of the institutionalisation of research. Although the aim of informed consent is presumably to protect respondents, informing them of the possibility of harm in advance and inviting them to withdraw if they so desire, it also effectively releases the institution or funding agency from any liability and gives control of the research process to the researcher.
>
> (Fine *et al.* 2000: 113)

Furthermore, as Pring (2000) notes, each research situation needs to be considered in its own light and decisions about codes of practice and what might be acceptable made on a case-by-case basis. Thus some research questions and settings may justify covert approaches because otherwise the research would never get done and information that may be valuable for the pursuit of social justice would not be obtained.

Codes of practice, although they are undoubtedly of value, can have the effect of absolving researchers if their research has unintended or unexpected negative consequences. Can this really be considered to be moral research practice? Or is moral research practice a chimera? It is certainly the case that researchers from different traditions and with different theoretical and political positions have different conceptions of what constitutes moral research (for a review, see Christians 2000). In Pring's terms, they have different characters and dispositions and much depends on whether the emphasis is placed on outcomes or processes. This emphasis has implications for the sorts of methodologies and methods that researchers choose or are required to use, and the sorts of stories that the types of information these variously yield enable them to tell. Our view is that life histories help explain how researchers come to particular positions and so, at this point, it is appropriate to move on and offer our own histories, as they relate to our careers as educational researchers, as examples. We will present our accounts separately and then offer some observations on them, which we believe illustrate our thesis about the importance of collective memory.

Towards a notion of educational research as moral practice: A life-history approach

Pat's story

It wasn't until I began thinking about my involvement in and with educational research that I realized the extent to which my whole life – educational, professional, personal – has been affected by various projects and the moral values and commitments underlying them. It quickly became clear that compiling and then representing my life history as it relates to educational research was not going to be straightforward, owing to the sheer complexity and interrelatedness of things. Nor was it going to be possible to mention everything, let alone give the level of detail I'd like to. Selection is necessary and inevitably I'm going to choose the examples that fit the story I want to tell in the most economical manner.

I believe that if, throughout my school career from 1960 to 1974, I hadn't been a 'subject' in a massive educational action research project, my life, in all of its aspects, would have been very different. The project was the 'Leicestershire Experiment' (Mason 1970; Fairbairn 1980). It was very much of its time, growing out of and being part of that optimistic post-war social thrust towards a better society – a moral quest for sure. This wasn't small-scale research but a massive reorganization of one local authority's educational services, with the overall democratic aim of widening access to education. Thus, and for example: comprehensive secondary schools were introduced at a very early stage compared with in other parts of the country; community colleges were established; curriculum reform and development was encouraged and supported; school counsellors were employed to attend to students' emotional and personal needs; ideas about learning environments were given expression in innovative architecture; hierarchies of all kinds (e.g. curricular, pupil–teacher relationships) were challenged; the arts, and in particular music, were given equal status with academic work; and the democratic involvement of students and teachers in the running of schools was explored.

The consequences for me were many and varied. My schooldays were golden, my experiences rich. I was able to develop and flourish. I was given a sense of my unique worth. It may not have been like that for everyone, I know. But I was a working-class child from a family that was incredibly loving and supportive but that had no tradition of higher education and no understanding about how the system worked. To some extent, because I was in Leicestershire, that background didn't matter. Also, and probably more important for me, there was no 11-plus to fail, and fail it I would have done because I had, and have, a problem with maths. As it was, I went into the same sort of secondary education as everyone else did. Sure, I was limited because of my lack of cultural capital, but the experiences I had at my various schools went some way to compensate.

My school had an open sixth form, underpinned by the philosophy that students develop at different rates and that lack of success at an early stage was not necessarily predictive of lack of ability. Although I only got four 'O' level equivalent passes, I was allowed to take the three 'A' levels that would have been denied me in many other schools and, consequently, I was able to go to college.

Looking back I can see that some of the ways in which the egalitarian philosophy was expressed and realized were perhaps, mistaken. For instance, the headteacher had taken the decision that, wherever possible, pupils would be entered for Mode 3 CSEs rather than 'O' levels. Teachers themselves designed the syllabi for, and assessed, these exams and the head's belief, shared by many, although not all of the staff, was that the curriculum and pedagogy would be more meaningful, more exciting if this were the case. Not only that, but the teachers would benefit personally and professionally from the level of autonomy and involvement they provided. By and large, my experience of the courses I followed suggested that he was right and a lot of what I learnt has stayed with me. Out in the wider world though, CSEs were not good currency. This wasn't such a problem for those going on to take 'A' levels (a far lower percentage in those days than now) as it was for the students who left school at this stage.

Then there was the decision to let the sixth formers have a designated smoking room! With hindsight, that is almost unbelievable, but at the time it was seen as being acceptable. Pupils at all levels of the school were full members of school councils and freedom to smoke, to wear whatever you liked, to call teachers by their first names, to challenge 'infringements' of liberty, were all understood to be fundamental rights. The headteacher's personal Quaker values influenced how he managed the school, but he was only operating within the local authority's vision. Indeed, compared with how this vision was interpreted and realized at a neighbouring school, Countesthorpe College (see Watts 1977), Mr F. could have been considered to have been extremely circumspect.

As I have noted, traditional hierarchies were questioned and this included relationships between pupils and teachers. It was usual for sixth-form pupils and young teachers to meet socially and, consequently, romantic and sexual relationships did develop. There are, of course, ethical and moral questions around this issue, but it happened (see Sikes 2000; Goodson and Sikes 2001). It happened to me, and my history teacher became my boyfriend. Like so many others of his generation (see Sikes 1988), this young man was full of the idealism of the 1960s. He saw education as an immediate route to social change and was keen to become involved in curriculum research and development and innovative pedagogy. When the opportunity arose for him to train to teach the Humanities Curriculum Project (HCP), he took it (Schools Council/Nuffield 1970).

He started attending conferences and got to know Lawrence Stenhouse,

Jean Rudduck and other academics and teachers involved in HCP and the work of the Centre for Applied Research in Education (CARE) more generally. He became a member of working parties and took part in a study focusing on teacher dissemination (Rudduck and Stenhouse 1979). Of greatest significance though, for him and for me as it turned out, was his involvement in the SSRC/Gulbenkian project 'The problems and effects of teaching about race relations' (see Sikes and Sheard 1978; Sikes 1979; Stenhouse *et al.* 1982) and his membership of the National Association for Teaching About Race Relations (NARTAR).

During this time, the mid-1970s, we were living in the West Riding of Yorkshire, another radical local education authority under the directorship of Sir Alec Clegg. David was teaching in an innovative humanities department and I was a student at a teacher training college. Whenever there were HCP or NARTAR meetings or conferences, I would go along and listen to and join in the talk about educational issues that went on into the early hours. I remember sitting in a bar, complaining to Lawrence Stenhouse that I'd got to write an essay in support of objectives-based teaching and of how he helped me to think through a critique. I got an A, I recall!

My links with CARE brought me in to contact with a particular philosophy of, and approach to, educational research. But this wasn't all, because back at college I was fortunate to have a sociology of education lecturer who was a graduate of Ruskin College and who was tremendously enthusiastic about, and very excited by, the 'new sociology' (Young 1971). He passed on that enthusiasm and over the four years that he taught me, Rex Daine introduced me to the work of authors such as C. Wright Mills, W.I. Thomas, Paulo Friere, Erving Goffman, Howard Becker, Basil Bernstein and Pierre Bourdieu.

By the time I came to leave college, I was fascinated by the sociology and philosophy of education, but I wasn't very keen on becoming a schoolteacher. Luckily for me, NARTAR needed a research assistant to 'do something to produce some teacher training materials' from the hours of tape-recordings of classroom discussions that had been collected as part of the 'Problems and effects of teaching about race relations' project. It may have been nepotism, but I got the job and, in September 1979, I went to work at CARE and eventually produced a book (Sikes 1979) that was used by NARTAR members in training courses.

While I was at CARE, Lawrence would give me things to read. I remember a whole batch of papers from an AERA conference, including one by Bob Stake on 'Telling it like it was', advocating honesty in writing up research. Then there were the seminars and the conversations in the corridor. Louis Smith was there on a study leave and so I came to hear about the Kensington ethnography. During the year I was there, I met so many people, staff, students and visitors whose names were then, or are now, well-known in particular educational research circles (Jean Rudduck, Harry

Torrance, David Hopkins, Nigel Norris, Saville Kushner, Clem Adelman, Rob Walker, Barry MacDonald, John Elliott and Helen Simon are just a few).

Lawrence was a facilitator, an enabler, a sponsor. He gave me the confidence to believe that I could have a career in educational research. He also wrote a mean reference and so, after CARE, I went to Leeds University's School of Education, on an SSRC (now ESRC) studentship.

In my application, I'd proposed a study of teacher motivation at a time when promotion prospects looked likely to be diminished as a result of falling school rolls. The supervisor I was allocated to, Peter Tomlinson, was a psychologist with a relatively traditional positivist approach to research, although he had an interest in the social psychological approaches of people like George Kelly and Rom Harre.

In those days and in that institution, there was no training programme specifically for doctoral students, but my supervisor directed me to attend a master's level class that he taught on statistics tests. I went along but found the work difficult to understand. Nor was I convinced that statistical interpretations could appropriately address the questions and issues I was interested in, because these concerned subjective perceptions that I didn't think could be easily quantified.

However, my supervisor told me that, if I was to get my PhD, I had to do 'proper' research: in other words, research within the positivist paradigm, research which yielded sufficient data to perform statistical tests and to allow and support generalizations. If I did this, he said, I could bring in some of the 'soft qualitative stuff' I was so keen on! So I devised a questionnaire with codable items and used SPSS, as well as compiling case studies and conducting interviews, and eventually got my doctorate (Sikes 1986).

I had heeded my supervisor's advice and included quantitative data but I'd reversed the balance he suggested because, as I did more life-history interviewing and ethnographic case study work, I'd become convinced that subjective perceptions best fitted my view of the social world and made it easier for me to make an interpretation that I found meaningful. I'd also come to feel that inviting people to give their view, rather than asking them to fit their experiences into a framework I'd constructed, was inherently more respectful of them and of their opinions. And, most significantly for how my career subsequently developed, I'd reached the conclusion that to begin to understand social events and people's perceptions and experiences of them, 'one must confront biography' (Bullough 1998: 24). Life history seemed, and seems, to me to be the most appropriate approach to social and, therefore, educational issues (as it was so unequivocally put so long ago, 'life records, as complete as possible, constitute the *perfect* type of sociological material': Thomas and Znaniecki 1918–1920: 1832–3). It was with this conviction that, in September 1982, I went to work with Peter

Woods and Lynda Measor on a life-history research project looking at teachers' experiences of teaching as career (Sikes *et al.* 1985). Through Peter I got 'plugged in' to a network of ethnographers who met each year at a conference at St Hilda's College, Oxford. Thus it was I came to know the work of people like Colin Lacey, Sara Delamont, Bob Burgess, June Purvis, Jenny Nias, Martin Lawn, Andy Hargreaves, Stephen Ball, Mairtin Mac an Ghail, Sandra Acker, Martyn Hammersley and, of course, Ivor Goodson.

At this point I am going to end, although there are still twenty years to go to reach the point at which I'm writing. Twenty years in which I've used life history to investigate such topics as: teachers' experiences of imposed change of various kinds (curricular, organizational, managerial); the impact of parenthood on teachers; what it is like to be a teacher of particular school subjects; the process of becoming a teacher; teachers and gender, 'race', sexuality, social class and religion-related issues and experiences; how life history can be a powerful tool for personal and professional development. Twenty years in which I've been a schoolteacher, a contract researcher, an evaluator, a teacher trainer, a lecturer. Twenty years in which I've met and worked with people whose research interests and commitments have broadened my understandings and awareness, especially with regard to social justice issues – my eight-year friendship and professional collaboration with Barry Troyna is paramount in my thoughts here. Twenty years in which I've had time to reflect on and explore issues to do with research methods and methodologies and their application in educational settings. Twenty years in which my overriding and underlying motivation and focus has been the pursuit of social justice through education in general, and educational research in particular, because it is with regard to the latter that I have been able to pass something on, effect some change, make some impact, however slight.

My career as an educational researcher, the values and beliefs that I hold and which inform my practice, have roots in the experiences I've had and the influences I've been exposed to. In this brief extract from my life history as it relates to educational research, I have tried to give a sense of where I am coming from. What I haven't gone into, for reasons to do with space and focus, is my faith, which continues to be a significant influence on my conceptualization of social justice and my views on educational research as moral practice. And there are other areas of my life that also inform and articulate with these notions – my experiences and understandings as a parent, as a school governor, as a reader of newspapers and watcher of television, for example. Then there are the experiences and views of friends, family members, research informants, colleagues and acquaintances. All of these have contributed to my perspectives and understandings of research as moral practice.

Ivor's story[1]

I grew up in a family that was both proud of its place and committed to a vision of progress for the community in general. These were not especially unusual characteristics in poor communities at the time, although writing them down feels somewhat 'golden age'. This was, after all, the time of the 'long march of Labour'. A time that is now hard to imagine, let alone 're-enter' (Goodson 1995c).

My father was a gas fitter; my mother worked in a wartime munitions factory. My father was the youngest of thirteen children (he was lucky enough to be preceded by twelve sisters); his father was an unskilled labourer, mostly unemployed, his mother took in laundry. My mother was one of six children and had two sisters and three brothers. Her father and mother ran a workingman's cafe in Reading. It was while serving breakfast one morning in 1929 that she met my father. They married in 1932 and went to live in a working-class suburb of Reading called Woodley. My father was involved with the Gas Fitters Union; in 1945, both parents voted for a Labour government committed to bringing a better deal for working people and their children. This government was to have a substantial effect on my schooling. In 1949, I went to a school attached to the Church of England; it was very ill-resourced, having no textbooks, qualified teachers or separate classrooms (just one huge room with curtains across). I can still vividly recall the 'earth closets' that passed as toilets. At the time, I could not read or write. But the new Labour government had initiated a vigorous campaign to build new 'county primary schools'. So in 1950, I left the earth closets behind, to go to Loddon County Primary School. At the time, I still could not read but, given the ready supply of books and the qualified teachers, soon learnt through the efforts of some very committed teachers, concerned to spread learning to all. I passed the 11-plus examination three years later.

The 'grammar school' to which I was directed was a long way away from my village and I had to travel by bus and train or, in summer, undertake a long bicycle ride. This was only the beginning of a process that seemed calculated to take me away from my family and my culture. Within the school many features jarred with my cultural experiences. I was a ten-year-old child adrift in a very alien world. In retrospect, the major vehicle of alienation was the school curriculum – Latin, Greek, ancient history, grammar, English literature, physics, chemistry, and so on. A classical curriculum utterly divorced from my experience of the world. Like so many of my peers – as was well documented by David Hargreaves (1968) and Colin Lacey (1970) – I settled near the bottom of the class. In 1959, I took nine 'O' level examinations and passed one, history. That summer, I went to work in a potato crisp factory with three of my mates from Woodley.

It looked, therefore, that I had merely been 'learning to labour', but then came divine intervention. My history teacher must have been pleased with his singular success at teaching me something (compared with the other eight subject teachers), for he arrived at the crisp factory in September and announced that I should return to school. Shouting above the noise of the factory I said I might do just that. School had begun to look desirable. So I worked hard, passed a few 'O' levels that year and joined the sixth form. In due course, I passed my 'A' level examinations and went off to London University. I did an economics degree (specializing in economic history) and, having done quite well in the final examinations, was offered a research studentship at the London School of Economics. For four years I fumbled away at a doctorate on Irish immigrants in Victorian England and in my final year became a lecturer at what is now Kingston University.

I never settled to this work and began spending increasing amounts of time back home in Woodley. This still felt like home. This was where my friends and family were. Moreover, the grammar schools were about to be replaced by comprehensive schools and the word in the pubs and clubs of Woodley was that this would offer an education to my class of people that would be of more interest and relevance than Latin, Greek and ancient history. My friends spent a lot of time talking about all this as a political strategy of hope.

In 1965, the Labour government announced its plans to establish comprehensive schools for everyone. More or less there and then, I decided to stop wasting my time studying Victorian England and lecturing in higher education to the 'sons and daughters of gentlefolk' and to get involved in teaching in comprehensive schools. I applied to go to the Institute of Education in London to train to be a teacher.

After 15 years of schooling and university being taught by people from another class about subjects utterly disconnected from anything I had experienced, suddenly everything changed. The tutors were mostly from a similar background and the subject was essentially *our* experience of education and culture. The sociology department in 1969 was in a real sense like coming home (with all the tensions and ambivalences carried therein). And it was to know, for perhaps the first time, that learning did not have to be alienating, that connectedness was possible. It was also to likewise learn that disconnectedness was often socially constructed.

To experience what 'could be' in terms of social science scholarship was also then to learn what was 'not allowed to be'. To learn what 'could be' in terms of pedagogic discourse and relationships was to be shown with unforgettable clarity how curriculum, culture and class were irrevocably enmeshed. For a few years (in the social democratic moment that followed 1968), in the sociology department a 'contradictory gap' was opened up. During that time, work on 'knowledge and control' proceeded not only at the scholarly level, but also at the level of the lived experience for those who clustered around the tables of Taviton Street and of the local pubs. Many conversations have stayed with me since. One I remember was between me, Rob Walker (see Goodson and Walker 1991), who was finishing a research degree with Bernstein, and Basil himself. It started in Taviton Street with a long argument about styles of pedagogy and the comprehensive school. It then moved along the street to the Marlborough pub where it went on for five hours. A good deal of the discussion turned on Basil's use of the term 'transmission' in some of his work (see Bernstein 1971: 47). This we argued was to use the language of dominant pedagogies while speaking of other visions.

In the cold light of day though, I found myself nagging away at what had been said. Through the mists of the Marlborough, a programme of study began tentatively to emerge.

Bernstein's work in particular showed me that there were modes of academic study where the everyday experiences of ordinary pupils and people might be investigated. In short, where my experience of life and my intellectual questions about that experience might be finally reconnected. But, just as in a previous period of my life, I had to abandon my intellectual interests to pass examinations; now once again, I had to abandon an academic career as a university lecturer so that self and study might be reinvested with some degree of authenticity (Goodson 1995b).

I saw the newly organizing comprehensive schools as the place where I wanted to work. In due course, I worked at Countesthorpe in Leicestershire during its early years, and later at Stantonbury in Milton Keynes. In this way, my own class background and experience might engage with that of my pupils in a 'common language' of dialogue between teacher and taught. For the new generation of pupils from working homes, there might be something beyond the pervasive alienation I had experienced at school, an alienation intimately related to the form and content of the traditional grammar school curriculum. In the event, comprehensive schools often found themselves teaching many of these traditional grammar school subjects. As I have described elsewhere (Goodson 1993), new subjects faced a bitterly contested battle for acceptance and the traditional subjects normally maintained their supremacy. It became important to understand the problems of status, resources and power, which underlay and underpinned school subjects.

The battle for the supremacy of the 'traditional subjects' in the comprehensive school was a battle to reinstate grammar school priorities within the 'common school'. It was, of course, also a battle about social distribution, about which social groups would gain priority and preferment in the contest for credentials.

The same battle was replayed in the period when a 'national curriculum' was defined. This time, the traditional subjects were given legislated supremacy, and many of those subjects devised with a comprehensive clientele in mind were marginalized. In due course, it could be claimed, the comprehensive experiment had failed.

One of the most interesting ways to come to understand these contests over school subject destinies, and over the social mission of schooling, is by studying teachers' and indeed students' life histories. Our own brief life histories illustrate how each life is a map of changing social priorities and possibilities. It is true that we 'make our own history', but not 'in circumstances of our own choosing'. The life history allows us to watch the balance between 'making' and being 'made'. In schooling, we see how possibilities open up and are then circumscribed; how what at one time can be seen to be constructed is later accepted as normative and 'given'.

Discussion

Twelve years separate us in age. There are many and fundamental differences between us. And yet . . . And yet we have passed through similar spaces and times, which have had similar impacts upon our notions of, and commitment to, educational research as moral practice. With regard to the coincidence that we were both in Leicestershire schools in the early and exciting days of the comprehensive project, it is interesting how Pat, as a pupil, can be seen to inhabit some of the moral spaces that Ivor was aiming to facilitate through his agency as a teacher. That we were not even in the same school does not necessarily diminish the impact of the jointly experienced collective mission of all those others like us working in education at that time. And similarly, throughout the subsequent years in the spaces that we have occupied as educational researchers, ideas about research as moral practice have been shared, passed on and developed.

In conclusion, our thoughts on moral research practice can be summarized as follows:

- Moral practice, most commonly, is grounded in the life trajectory and generational sense of mission that educational researchers develop. Understanding and refining the 'moral career' of educational researchers, therefore, becomes a central concern, particularly given the absence of such concerns within marketized models of educational reform.
- Moral practice seldom originates in the marketized, consumer-oriented model of education because, despite the rhetoric that a healthy economy is better for everyone, it doesn't seem to work like that. Markets are not concerned with moral issues, but with profit. They are not in the social justice business.
- We think research practice that fails to give individual, personal, subjective perceptions and experiences the primacy they should have in research that is about the social world is not likely to pursue a moral mission, because the social and the individual are so deeply interlinked. This is returning to the relationship between public matters and private concerns.

- We think much research practice is based on the understanding that, as long as a code of ethics is adhered to, then it is 'moral'. In fact, this view reduces moral concerns to the procedural: a convenient form of methodological reductionism.
- We think research practice is immoral if it is mechanistic and applied in a technical manner without regard for the specific conditions and circumstances of each particular research context.
- We think research practice is immoral if researchers do not own their involvement in the process and if they claim value neutrality.
- We think research practice is immoral if it fails to acknowledge and build on the lessons of the past – if collective memories are erased or ignored in the process of undertaking the research.

These conclusions flow from the concern to elucidate the relationship between our own lives, life experiences and life stories, and our research practice. In general, we take the view that such 'interior reflexivity' is a better anchor for moral practice than the exterior guidelines currently articulated through educational reform initiatives. We recognize that there will be a dialectic between the two, but favour 'interior reflexivity' over external mandating when it comes to matters of moral definition and decision.

In a sense, what we have tried to do here is bear witness to the past. By happenstance we have lived through some particularly heady times in terms of human optimism and the quest for social justice. Critics may say that we are simply getting old and slipping into Golden Age reminiscing, but we don't think so. Our aim has not been to evoke a nostalgia for times past that fails to recognize the ideological forces that were at work then, creating myths as well as providing a basis for memories (see McCulloch *et al.* 2000: 42–55). Indeed, we are conscious that, in writing this chapter and in selecting some while omitting other aspects of our experiences as we see them relating to notions of research as moral practice, we are exploiting the political nature and potential of memory: both our own personal memories and the collective memory of a particular group of researchers (and other researchers and groups thereof clearly have different memories influencing their perspectives and positions). Tittler points out that,

> memories are neither randomly formed nor immutable. The collective act of remembering remains a dynamic and highly subjective process, in which deliberate reconstruction is even more important than random recollection. What each group or generation remembers depends very considerably on the requirements of its own time and place, especially as conceived by its leaders.
>
> (Tittler 1997: 283–4)

We certainly do not see ourselves as leaders, but we do think it is important to hold on to memories of the 1960s and 1970s when there was considerable support for, and attempts to realize, democratic education – and to reflect on why this was seen as being so dangerous. As Pierre Nora (1989) warns, 'history is perpetually suspicious of memory and its true mission is to suppress and destroy it' (p. 9). Thus, to forget would, we think, be in itself, immoral.

Note

1 The section on Ivor's story in this volume is a modified version of the related section in 'Basil Bernstein and aspects of the sociology of the curriculum', in P. Atkinson, B. Davies and S. Delamont (eds) *Discourse and Reproduction: Essays in Honor of Basil Bernstein* (1995).

References

Ball, S. (2001) Performativities and fabrications in the education economy: towards the performance society, in D. Gleeson and C. Husbands (eds) *The Performing School: Managing Teaching and Learning in a Performance Context*. London: Routledge Falmer.

Bernstein, B. (1971) On the classification and framing of educational knowledge, in M. Young (ed.) *Knowledge and Control*. London: Collier Macmillan.

Bullough, R. (1998) Musings on life writing: biography and case study in teacher education, in C. Kridel (ed.) *Writing Educational Biography: Explorations in Qualitative Research*. New York: Garland.

Christians, C. (2000) Ethics and politics in qualitative research, in N. Denzin and Y. Lincoln (eds) *Handbook of Qualitative Research*, 2nd edn. Thousand Oaks, CA: Sage.

Ellis, C. and Bochner, A. (2000) Autoethnography, personal narrative, reflexivity, in N. Denzin and Y. Lincoln (eds) *Handbook of Qualitative Research*, 2nd edn. Thousand Oaks, CA: Sage.

Fairbairn, A. (ed.) (1980) *The Leicestershire Plan*. London: Heinemann.

Fine, M., Weiss, L., Wesen, S. and Wong, L. (2000) For whom? Qualitative research, representations and social responsibilities, in N. Denzin and Y. Lincoln (eds) *Handbook of Qualitative Research*, 2nd edn. Thousand Oaks, CA: Sage.

Flyvbjerg, B. (2001) *Making Social Science Matter: Why Social Inquiry Fails and How it can Succeed Again*. Cambridge: Cambridge University Press.

Goodson, I. (1992) Studying teachers' lives: an emergent field of inquiry, in I. Goodson (ed.) *Studying Teachers' Lives*. London: Routledge.

Goodson, I. (1993) *School Subjects and Curriculum Change*, 3rd edn. London: Falmer Press.

Goodson, I. (1995a) The story so far: the personal and the political, in J.A. Hatch and R. Wisniewski (eds) *Life History and Narrative*. London: Falmer Press.

Goodson, I. (1995b) *The Making of Curriculum: Collected Essays*, 2nd edn. London: Falmer Press.

Goodson, I. (1995c) Basil Bernstein and aspects of the sociology of the curriculum, in P. Atkinson, B. Davies and S. Delamont (eds) *Discourse and Reproduction: Essays in Honor of Basil Bernstein*. Cresskill, N.J.: Hampton Press.

Goodson, I. (1997) The educational researcher as a public intellectual, *The Lawrence Stenhouse Memorial Lecture, British Educational Research Association*, York, September.

Goodson, I. and Sikes, P. (2001) *Life History Research in Educational Settings*. Buckingham: Open University Press.

Goodson, I. and Walker, R. (1991) *Biography, Identity and Schooling: Episodes in Educational Research*. London: Falmer.

Halbwachs, M. (1992) *Collective Memory*. Chicago, IL: University of Chicago Press.

Hargreaves, D. (1968) *Social Relations in the Secondary School*. London: Routledge & Kegan Paul.

Hertz, R. (ed.) (1997) *Reflexivity and Voice*. Thousand Oaks, CA: Sage.

Kuhn, T. (1962) *The Structure of Scientific Revolutions*. Chicago, IL: University of Chicago Press.

Lacey, C. (1970) *Hightown Grammar*. Manchester: Manchester University Press.

McCulloch, G., Helsby, G. and Knight, P. (2000) *The Politics of Professionalism: Teachers and the Curriculum*. London: Continuum.

MacIntyre, A. (1981) *After Virtue: A Study in Moral Theory*. London: Duckworth.

MacIntyre, A. (1989) *Three Rival Versions of Moral Enquiry: Encyclopaedia, Genealogy, and Tradition*. London: Duckworth.

MacLure, M. (1993) Mundane autobiography: some thoughts on self-talk in research contexts, *British Journal of Sociology of Education*, 14: 373–84.

Mason, S. (ed.) (1970) *In Our Experience: The Changing Schools of Leicestershire*. Harlow: Longmans.

Maynard, M. (1993) Feminism and the possibilities of a postmodern research practice, *British Journal of Sociology of Education*, 14(3): 327–31.

Measor, L. and Sikes, P. (1992) Visiting lives: ethics and methodology in life history research, in I. Goodson (ed.) *Studying Teachers' Lives*. London: Routledge.

Mykhalovskiy, E. (1997) Reconsidering 'table talk': critical thoughts on the relationship between sociology, autobiography and self-indulgence, in R. Hertz (ed.) *Reflexivity and Voice*. Thousand Oaks, CA: Sage.

Nora, P. (1989) Between memory and history: les lieux de memoire, *Representations*, 26: 7–25.

Pring, R. (2000) *Philosophy of Educational Research*. London: Continuum.

Rosen, H. (1998) *Speaking from Memory: The Study of Autobiographical Discourse*. Stoke-on-Trent: Trentham.

Rudduck, J. and Stenhouse, L. (1979) *A Study in the Dissemination of Action Research*. Norwich: CARE.

Schools Council/Nuffield Humanities Project (1970) *The Humanities Project: An Introduction*. London: Heinemann.

Sennett, R. (1999) *The Corrosion of Character*. New York: W.W. Norton.

Sikes, P. (1979) *Teaching about Race Relations*. Norwich: CARE (reprinted 1984).

Sikes, P. (1986) The mid-career teacher: adaptation and motivation in a contracting secondary school system (unpublished doctoral dissertation), University of Leeds.

Sikes, P. (1988) The 68ers, communication to the British Educational Research Association, University of East Anglia, Norwich, September.

Sikes, P. (1997) *Parents Who Teach: Stories from Home and from School*. London: Cassell.

Sikes, P. (2000) Dangerous liaisons? When male teachers and female pupils fall in love. Unpublished paper, University of Warwick.

Sikes, P. and Sheard, D. (1978) Teaching for better race relations?, *Cambridge Journal of Education*, 8(2–3): 165–72.

Sikes, P., Measor, L. and Woods, P. (1985) *Teacher Careers: Crises and Continuities*. Lewes: Falmer Press.

Sikes, P., Troyna, B. and Goodson, I. (1996) Talking lives: a conversation about life history, *Taboo: The Journal of Culture and Education*, 1: 35–54.

Stenhouse, L., Verma, G., Wild, R. and Nixon, J. (1982) *Teaching about Race Relations: Problems and Effects*. London: Routledge.

Thomas, W. and Znaniecki, F. (1918–1920) *The Polish Peasant in Europe and America*, 2nd edn. Chicago, IL: University of Chicago Press.

Tierney, W. (2000) Undaunted courage: life history and the postmodern challenge, in N. Denzin and Y. Lincoln (eds) *Handbook of Qualitative Research*, 2nd edn. Thousand Oaks, CA: Sage.

Tittler, R. (1997) Reformation, civic culture and collective memory in English provincial towns, *Urban History*, 24(3): 283–300.

Watts, J. (ed.) (1977) *The Countesthorpe Experience*. London: Allen & Unwin.

Young, M. (ed.) (1971) *Knowledge and Control*. London: Collier Macmillan.

4 | The virtues and vices of an educational researcher

Richard Pring

Introduction

Educational researchers are becoming increasingly conscious of the ethical dimension of their research. Unlike medical and nursing researchers, they do not yet have their 'ethical committees' to check the acceptability of research proposals. But the British Educational Research Association and the American Educational Research Association have drawn up codes of conduct – principles and rules that should guide the research from an ethical point of view. Furthermore, it is now usually expected that research theses will explain what the ethical issues are in the conduct of the research and how the researchers ensured that appropriate standards of conduct were maintained.

This chapter examines this ethical dimension and questions whether it is sufficient to think in terms of principles, codes and rules. It may be more important, from an ethical point of view, to consider much more carefully the virtues of the researcher than the principles he or she espouses. In so arguing, I first examine four examples and, in the light of these, reflect on the role of principles and virtues in the exercise of research.

Examples

The undercover bouncer

In the recent book, *Danger in the Field: Risk and Ethics in Social Research*, David Calvey (2000) described how, in his undercover research to explore the 'cultural practice, work culture and social organisation' of club bouncers,[1] he secretly tape-recorded conversations and recorded assaults, drug-taking and other crimes. His role as a researcher had to be disguised – discovery might literally have been fatal. Therefore, what he learnt (and then reported) was gained from confidential conversations and by the concealment both of his identity and of the purposes of the research. His justification (the moral argument, if you like) was that, first, he was contributing to an understanding of violence in society and, second, the deceptive method adopted was the only way in which he could attain that worthwhile objective.

The toilet ethnographer (or 'undercover ethnographer', if you like)

Consider a second case. Some years ago an established researcher investigated the classroom ethos of three middle schools. Entry to those schools required gaining the confidence of the relevant teachers and the headteachers. He described the steps he took to maintain secrecy and unobtrusiveness – for example, always writing up his observations behind the locked door of the toilet. But the publication of the book, though steps had been taken to anonymize the schools and the teachers, greatly upset one of the teachers who recognized herself in reading the book and took offence at the implicit criticism of her teaching. The headteacher told me that, in consequence, he would allow no more researchers into his school.

The democratic researcher

A third example is that of a researcher who took seriously the feelings of those being researched and negotiated agreement of what was permissible data and what was a permissible analysis of that data, prior to publication, before they entered into the report. It was agreed that a significant portion of the data would not be made public (for example, what the teacher had said when interviewed) and, therefore, could not enter into the analysis. This meant, of course, gaps in the overall picture and distorted conclusions. But in one sense this did not matter, because the process of negotiating the evidence and the conclusions was so prolonged that no report was ever written. However, the researcher justified the procedure of lengthy negotiation by reference to the benefit received by the school in going through the process, even though that process never reached any conclusions. (The researcher resisted one moral temptation – namely, to draw conclusions that were correct in the light of the evidence but which the sensitivities of the teachers had prevented from becoming public.)

The contract researcher

A fourth example is that of a researcher desperate to win further major research contracts from the government sponsor. Here, as is often the case, short-term contract researchers depended on a successful proposal for their continuation in employment. As with most government-funded projects, there were no absolute criteria for evaluating the success of the overall project. Most major projects of this kind (Education Action Zones, Fast Track Teachers, etc.) have a mixture of outcomes. Nevertheless, the researcher knew that there was a limit to how much criticism would be acceptable to his sponsor and, in any case, there was a team of experienced spin doctors (called the Press Office) to gainsay the research if the need arose. Experienced contract researchers realize that, with regard to research into policy, they are operating within a political context with an ideologically driven programme. The researcher in this case, therefore, distinguished between private advice and public documentation – between that which would be private to the government and that which would be open to the public. The public document, therefore, blunted its criticisms and thereby failed to contribute to a truly balanced debate on the issues. But the researcher claimed that, first, he did influence policy (which could not have been the case had he been less pragmatic and subtle in presenting the conclusions); second, he did receive another large grant and his research officer continued to feed his young family.

Reflecting on the examples

Moral dilemmas that arise in research are often dealt with by appeal to certain general principles. These are then translated into codes of conduct of research. The British Educational Research Association has developed its code, as has the American Educational Research Association. And this is to be highly commended. It is impossible to conceive of a moral life without implicit reference to a set of principles that are embodied within the moral practice. But that does not mean that one can, as it were, read off from that code or those principles what exactly one should do on any one occasion. There is no escaping moral deliberations – the complex judgements required for seeing, first, the relevance of particular principles or codes to this or that situation; second, the priority to be given to this or that principle when it is conflicting with another.

The examples above reflect the relevance of such moral deliberations or complex moral judgements. The person researching the culture of club bouncers (the first example above) was intentionally, yet secretly (and thus deceitfully), gathering information from unsuspecting bouncers. Indeed, it is likely that he engineered situations to get these accounts (gained their confidence, found safe places to talk, etc.). To be deceitful is, one might argue, a prima facie wrong. To engage in conversation with unsuspecting persons for ulterior motives that one takes care to hide (those motives being to publish what one hears and sees) would seem to be clearly wrong. But had he revealed his purposes, he would not have got the information and he might have been seriously harmed. Should he, then, not have engaged on the research? His argument was that the reasons were so important for the public good and for the general welfare that such deception was justified.

That, indeed, sounds plausible. But there is another dimension to the moral picture. As a result of the secrecy, there is no way in which the veracity of the conclusions could be checked. Remember that one general principle of good research is that conclusions are supported by evidence and that the relation of conclusion to evidence, and the evidence on which those conclusions are drawn, should be open to scrutiny – and might be considered acceptable only if they have withstood public criticism. Otherwise, educational research, to a much greater extent than, say, scientific research, would be dependent on the trustworthiness of the researchers. Are they the sort of person we can trust? (Do they pass the moral test?)

The second example, that of the 'toilet ethnographer' or 'undercover ethnographer' (whichever the Editors prefer), is again one where moral judgement is required. The researcher needs to weigh up the importance to his research of concealment and the likely effect that the results of the research would have on those researched into. Is this another case of deception? And, if so, then is it exactly the same as the previous case? In one sense it is, but in another it is not. It is not the same in the sense that the first case, but not the second, was revealing information of utmost importance for society. Moreover, secrecy (and deception) were crucial to the safety (indeed, continued existence) of the researcher. Same principles, but different context, requiring different deliberations about the application of principles. But could the second researcher have approached the research in a different way, recognizing the vulnerability of the persons researched into – and possibly respecting *their* interpretation of events (their conclusions from the data), which may not have been the same as those of the researcher? Indeed, how far can we understand what is going on in classrooms without respecting the understanding of the main agents within those classrooms? But this is hardly possible without the teachers' views being solicited.

The third example, that of the 'democratic researcher', takes these moral anxieties seriously. Judgements are made such that those being researched into must be brought to the centre of the picture. The *moral* ground for this is that any other course would show disrespect for them as persons. To research them through deceptive methods (as in the first two examples) would be to treat them as objects, things, not as persons worthy of respect. This 'respect for persons' (as in the sense of people not to be used for other people's ends) would seem to be the dominant principle. But more than that, the moral principle is also related to a view about the nature of knowledge – the tentativeness of any knowledge-claims, their openness to refinement and further criticism, the importance in reaching conclusions (even if temporary) which have withstood the widest range of possible criticism.

But there is a difficulty here. The importance of deliberation is recognized – indeed, espoused enthusiastically. And that deliberation takes place between the many people in the research – no longer divided between researcher and researched but united in a common partnership to discover the truth (which, of course, is often made elusive by the very complexity of the deliberations). A moral as well as a research bond is created, and the concept of negotiation (once intelligible in the world of business) takes on a moral force not recognized in the first two examples. But part of that moral force lies, too, in a view about the nature of knowledge, something which is seen to be constantly constructed and reconstructed.

The final example, that of the 'contract researcher', takes on yet a different dimension – different complexities in the moral debate. The researcher has two obligations that complicate the deliberation. The first obligation is to a long-term influencing of events in the light of research, which requires playing a political game abhorrent to the moral purist. But such would seem to be inescapable to those who walk the corridors of power. One is surrounded by the spinners and manipulators of knowledge. These are the lobbyists who carefully select one aspect of the research, ignoring the overall and balanced picture. There is the long-term aim, achievable through carefully explored short-term measures. Politics transforms the context of moral judgement.

But there is the second obligation – the obligation to the long-term well-being of the research team, ensuring contracts, enhancing its reputation, promoting its trustworthiness. There is a social as well as a political context of research, which, in its detail, escapes the direct application of high-level moral principles.

However, in all the examples there appears to be an inescapable dependence on the trustworthiness of the researcher – to exercise judgement in as impartial a manner as is possible, to conclude only those things that can be justified in the light of the evidence, to be open to the critical scrutiny of others where that is possible (and, where impossible, to imagine what that criticism might be).

What should be clear from a cursory consideration of the above four examples is the unavoidability of moral deliberation in considering the ethical dimension of research. Such deliberation does inevitably call upon or embody certain principles, but can by no means be simply the application of those principles. Different principles can be evoked. But there is *judgement* required in deciding upon the overriding principle and in deciding what element in one's practice relates to what principle. The context, for example, affects the amount of harm that might be considered tolerable and, indeed, what might be said to constitute harm. The context also affects the significance of the research to the wider public good. The context affects the extent to which secrecy might be equated with deceit. And the context affects the degree to which this piece of research should be seen as but part of a wider, more significant programme of research, such that moral imperfections might be allowed for the greater good of the whole.

It is necessary, therefore, to look more closely at the meaning and consequences of these considerations – first, at the role of principles in moral deliberations, but, second, at the moral requirement of research once one realizes that no set of principles (and thus no ethical code) can exhaustively shape the moral deliberation that inevitably researchers are caught in. The solution in my view lies in the return to 'moral virtue' appropriate to research, not an easy recommendation since the natural humility and modesty of most researchers would normally lead to their denial of having such virtues. Moreover, it is less easy to assess virtue than it is to assess research competence – or to pronounce a list of principles. Canon lawyers have to be clever, indeed subtle; they don't necessarily have to be virtuous.

Principles

Moral deliberation is often characterized as a response to the question, 'What ought I to do?' For much of the time, we do not have moral worries – getting up in the morning, preparing breakfast, choosing what to wear, and so on. Of course, one can see the *possibility* of moral conflict even in such everyday practices; my favourite but food-stained tie upsets my wife over the breakfast muesli, and no doubt this state of affairs could and should provoke some moral deliberations. But although any activity or practice can pose the question 'What ought I to do?' (where the 'ought' refers to an ethically significant situation rather than to a merely practical one), few (thank goodness) actually do.

But why is that the case? For most of our lives, our daily actions and relationships spring from the sort of people we are, the forms of life to which we belong with all its built-in norms and values. By being brought up in a particular society or social group, one absorbs the social rules and the feelings and dispositions which go with them, which are recognized by that group and which are appropriate to its particular form of life. It is not the case that the majority of people live in a constant state of existentialist angst. The question I want to ask is why the life of an educational researcher cannot be just like that? Why is there a need to spell out or make explicit codes of conduct, rules of procedure, principles of proper behaviour? Why can't we simply employ virtuous people with, of course, research skills?

The main reason is that the unreflecting but virtuous life is not sufficiently helpful when conflicts emerge, when underlying norms and values (previously only implicit) are challenged or eroded in the very social foundations of one's practice. It is then that the principles implicit in one's practice need to be more explicit. One then asks the question, 'What ought I to do?', seeking genuine reasons.

One sort of answer to the questions might be purely prudential or practical, namely, what particular action is most likely to achieve a particular end. But the question may be as much about the ends to be pursued as about the means of achieving those ends. The appropriate reasons for acting in one way rather than another, where those reasons focus on the values worth pursuing, are expressed in statements of principle. One appeals to principles in justifying an action. Moreover, principles by their nature reflect a universality of application. The *principle* of acting in this way rather than another does not depend upon my whims or wishes; anyone in like circumstances would be expected to act in a similar way. Thus, in asking the questions 'Why should I tell the interviewee the purpose of my research?' or 'Ought I to omit some of the more sensitive conclusions?', one would eventually appeal to some general principle, such as 'One ought to act in this way because such people have a right to know' or 'One should always tell the truth' or 'One should so treat others as one would wish them to treat oneself'.

One needs to distinguish between 'principles' and 'rules'. 'Rules' are more specific and less open to interpretation. There are rules for driving safely, such as 'Always drive on the left' and 'Never cross a double white line'. Thus, the government may lay down certain rules about the reporting of research that it has sponsored – let us say, the research should be sent confidentially to the Department of State and then, *only with the Department's permission*, might it be made accessible to the wider public. Such rules are of the kind 'In circumstances *x*, one must do *y*'. There is little ambiguity or openness to interpretation. But behind the rules for the conduct of research will be principles. Principles, related to the rules of safe driving, would be of the kind, 'So drive as to minimize the chance of causing an accident'. The rules for the conduct of government-sponsored research might be justified by reference to prescriptions such as 'The research report ought to be treated as the property of the sponsor' or 'The research ought to take account of the possible harm it might do to those who are researched into', which is then translated into the rules for the actual conduct of the research.

Principles, then, have the logic of general rules, but they embody the values appealed to in the establishment of the rules or in the questioning of the appropriateness of the rules on this or that occasion. There is a temptation, in recognizing the moral and political dilemmas over the conduct and the dissemination of research, to establish specific rules of conduct. But that would be a mistake. Here, as in any moral conflict, there is no way in which rules can legislate for every conceivable situation as, indeed, is shown in some of the examples given earlier. What specific rules could have anticipated the unique features of research into the criminal activity of club bouncers? Certainly, it is necessary to clarify principles, but these then need to be reflected on in the particular circumstances – in the full knowledge that other principles might also be evoked that would lead to more complex moral deliberation.

Moreover, a moment's reflection shows how unclear general principles are when it comes to their application. Thus 'maintaining confidentiality' might be narrowed down to the formal agreement not to mention what was said without the prior consent of the interviewee. But what about the case of the researcher talking to the club bouncers? No such agreement was entered into, but there was a deliberate deception (namely, the pursuit of information for a specific purpose while preventing the source of that information from knowing those purposes). Does that constitute a breaking of confidence? And is the situation so very different where the researcher engages in conversation and only subsequently (in the light of these private revelations) decides to use them for purposes of research or scholarship?

One needs to distinguish between those principles that are concerned with the consequences of one's actions (consequentialist) and those that express some general rules of behaviour, irrespective of the consequences (deontological). So, acting as to make people happier would be of the former kind; telling the truth or keeping confidences would be of the latter. It requires no great reflection to see how these different sorts of principles often conflict. Telling the truth can bring harm to others. Respect for individuals might entail a watering down of the research conclusions. The utilitarians wanted to judge the morality of all actions by reference to the extent to which those actions led to a greater sum of happiness than would otherwise be the case, even if that could be achieved only by the occasional lies or concealment of truth. Of course, it is not easy to calculate the total effect of any one action and, therefore, the utilitarians would argue a prima facie case for truth-telling and fairness as principles, which, generally speaking, lead to a happier state of affairs. But the clash of consequentialist and deontological ethical positions is clearly apparent in educational research. Calvey (2000) deceived his bouncers for the sake of the greater good to society, spelled out no doubt in terms of greater happiness as a result of less violence, drug trafficking, and so on. The researcher into middle schools put telling the truth (as he saw it) above the happiness of the individual teachers.

Such a *possible* conflict of irreconcilable principles can be resolved in one of four ways. First, the researcher simply does not recognize this to be a problem and pursues the research in a kind of moral vacuum. Research is cut off from moral life generally – it is put into an insulated occupational, amoral slot. Second, the researcher declares him or herself to be a deontologist or a consequentialist – and is always led by such principles to the exclusion of others (for example, one tells the truth whatever the consequences). Third, the researcher looks in vain for higher level principles to resolve the conflict. Fourth, the researcher recognizes that there is no solution other than, in most moral situations, through deliberation in which the different principles are pondered over within the particular context of the research. One situation is relevantly different from the next.

Nonetheless, the researcher should be aware of what the key principles are that enter into that deliberation – namely, principles concerned with the respect for other persons (maintaining confidentiality when promised, preserving their sense of dignity, treating them as having a valuable point of view); principles concerned with maximizing the happiness not only of the people immediately involved, but also of the wider community (balancing that happiness created against the unhappiness which might be caused); and third, principles concerned with the proper conduct of affairs irrespective of consequences (acting justly, keeping of promises, telling of the truth).

Let us look at these principles in greater detail. The principle that directs research would seem to be that of 'pursuing and telling the truth'. The purpose of undertaking research is, generally speaking, the generation of knowledge. The reasons for needing to know the truth concerns improvement of practice, development of policy, accountability of those in public and professional positions and, of course, the solution of problems raised by previous research. The production of knowledge requires access to data. Research, therefore, provides a prima facie case for the researchers having the right to such access. At the same time, there is a need for wider public access to those data and to the conclusions that researchers draw from them. One ought not to feel confident in the outcomes of research without this wider critical debate. Growth of knowledge comes through criticism.

The 'right to know' applies in particular when matters of public interest are concerned – for example, when large-scale interventions purport to improve standards or deal with a social evil. One can see why those in positions of power may wish to resist research or its conclusions. Research seeks to get at the truth where the truth might hurt. Research exposes the secrecy which, too often, permeates the conduct of affairs by public institutions such as schools, local authorities, government departments and committees. And researchers need a certain amount of courage to resist such powerful influences. However, policy makers (unless they have absolute trust in their spin doctors) should be keen to ensure that their decisions are informed by the most up-to-date knowledge and understanding and that the institutions are properly accountable. There would seem to be, therefore, a prima facie case for claiming the 'right to know'. Such research should remain independent of those who might benefit from or be disadvantaged by it, lest the conclusions drawn reflect the interests of the sponsors rather than the pursuit of the truth wherever that leads. Such is the importance of this right and this principle (namely, the 'right to know' and the principle that one should pursue and tell the truth) that they might be considered to be overriding, even when the research and its revelations damage the people and the institutions enquired into.

The justification for the principle of the right to know is implicit in John Stuart Mill's argument in his essay *On Liberty* for preserving and extending freedom of discussion:

> the peculiar evil of silencing the expression of an opinion is, that it is robbing the human race; posterity as well as the present generation; those who dissent from the opinion, still more than those who hold it. If the opinion is right, they are deprived of the opportunity of exchanging error for truth; if wrong, they lose, what is almost as great a benefit, the clearer perception and livelier impression of truth, produced by its collision with error.
>
> (Mill 1859: 142)

Accessibility of information is a precondition of a proper discussion of any opinion, policy or practice. Therefore, there is, on Mill's argument, a prima facie case for establishing the right to know as a basic one in any society, where the eradication of error or the greater clarity of the truth is valued, and thus the right – indeed, the obligation – to support and encourage independent research. There are no absolute certainties and thus, faced with the continual possibility of self-deception or of mistaken conclusions, any government or authority should welcome rather than spurn the well-researched criticism or proposal.

Therefore, the case for the right to know and the principle of pursuing the truth openly and independently (the ethical right and principle which should override all others and which should be supported through thick and thin) seems overwhelming. But those who have been engaged in research might well harbour some doubts.

First, the principle of constantly pursuing the truth (and supporting the connected right to know) is a principle, paradoxically, partly based on the premise that there are few areas where we can claim certainty. The growth of knowledge and understanding has constantly been at the expense of so-called certainties – bodies of 'knowledge' that were regarded as unquestionable. And the errors could be discovered only by constant vigilance – constant questioning of accepted truths. But the moral consequence of that lies in the appropriateness of modesty in the arrival at and promotion of the conclusions from research. All research and scholarship are littered with the corpses of authorities, of 'the last word' articles, of the definitive text that proved not to be definitive after all. Even in being guided by principles, the rational person needs to have the exercise of those principles softened by the virtues of modesty. The researcher might be wrong. If no researchers can ever provide the definitive word, then they must weigh the important but tentative nature of their research against the consequences of publishing it. What if they were wrong, and the consequences of their error were to cause harm to others? What if, given the political climate (with respect to, for example, effective schooling), they believed that the tentativeness of research findings would escape the less subtle politicians who quite clearly seek any scrap of evidence to support their policies? The researchers can, of course, put health warnings on their packets of research, but these (as we know from smoking) have little effect.

Second, there is the obvious tension between telling the truth and estimating the consequences of so telling. The insight into the school might harm the young teacher embarking on his or her career, or it might destroy the credibility of the school, thereby exacerbating the very problem revealed in the research. How much respect should be accorded to those who are most vulnerable in the light of the research? The obvious reply is 'It all depends . . .' – on the seriousness to the public good of the truth being revealed, on the degree of vulnerability of the potential victims and of their positions in the pecking order of power (presumably the much bigger salaries of headteachers are partly due to their greater responsibilities and accountability).

My third reservation lies in the role of confidentiality in the obtaining of data and in the interpretation of that data. As in the first example of Calvey (2000), the crucial evidence for the research would not have been obtainable had he observed the principle of voluntary informed consent. A certain deception was required. But then the purposes of the research were significant for the general good – the exposure of serious criminal activity. But cannot a similar argument be made for the significance of much educational research – the exposure of poor teaching, say, or the revelation of managerial incompetence at national or local levels? Where confidentiality is formally agreed, then the moral position is easier to resolve, but many aspects of the relationship between researcher and research are based on trust, not upon formal agreement. Virtues of loyalty, frankness, honesty, justice would be appealed to by the wronged person who was the object of the research.

How far, then, can one establish a set of principles for the conduct of research, bearing in mind the difficulties in translating these into a set of rules, and bearing in mind, too, the unavoidability of moral deliberation in reconciling conflicting principles or in seeing the applicability of this or that principle to this context?

There is a prima facie case for the right of access to whatever evidence will enable the researcher to get at the truth. But such a right should only be conceded where there are good reasons for conducting the research, and where there are grounds for believing that the research will be conducted honourably. (That is, there needs to be a trust in the researcher that can never be reduced to the faithful adherence to agreed principles and rules.) Hence, there would seem to be some very *general* rules that follow from the above analysis.

First, the researcher should set out clearly the *kinds* of knowledge required. Those being researched would have a right to know beforehand what in general terms the researchers would be looking for and for what purpose (with, however, already the exception to this principle in that research which needs to be conducted for the public good but which would not be possible were anyone to know its purpose). There would be the continuing opportunity to renegotiate the terms of the research contract as the research revealed new avenues for enquiry.

Second, the researcher would give access both to the data and to the conclusions drawn from those data, such that both might be questioned in the light of other data or of other possible conclusions. That is, there is the general principle that all should be done to enable and encourage public criticism of the conduct and conclusions of the research.

Third, the research should provide an opportunity for the right to reply from those who have participated in the research but who may believe that alternative conclusions could be supported by the data. The researcher, therefore, should be open to cross-examination by those at the receiving end of the research – the main purposes and objectives, the research methods, the political implications of the research, the data collected and the interpretations being put upon them. Such obligations arise from the ill-conceived nature of some research, and from the fact that all knowledge is both tentative and selective. There may be other perspectives and other interpretations of the data which should be considered.

Fourth, in terms of 'consequential principles', the researcher should take into account the possible ways in which research findings may be used. Research often appears in highly charged political contexts in which the findings are picked out selectively to support different sides of the political spectrum. Or the research may cause much harm and unhappiness to individuals or to the institution. One rule that is often derived from such a principle is that one should make the institutions or the individuals within them anonymous. But such a rule may be impossible to apply where the significance of the research may be related to the distinctive context.

The gap between high-level principles on the one hand and action on the other depends, as I have explained, on moral deliberation. But how one deliberates – what features of the situation one picks out as relevant, for example – depends on the general dispositions that incline one this way or that. A courageous person sees danger in a different way from the coward; the kind person will recognize redeeming features that the uncharitable fails to see; the loyal friend will focus on ways to help that mere companions will not detect. So, too, the ways in which researchers engage in moral deliberations depend on the sort of persons they are – the dispositions they have to act or respond in one way rather than another.

Virtues

There has been a tendency in moral philosophy, as in the conduct of research, to address what should be the principles of right action rather than the dispositions of the actor. And yet, as I have indicated in the previous section, it is not possible to proceed far without reference to such dispositions. On the whole, we act from character or from our dispositions to see, value and act in a certain way. Moral education, it might be argued, should concentrate more upon the nurturing of the virtues than upon the development of moral reasoning. By 'virtue' I mean the *disposition* to act appropriately in particular circumstances. There are moral virtues and intellectual virtues. Moral virtues are dispositions like courage, kindness, generosity of spirit, honesty, concern for justice.

Similarly with regard to the ethical dimension of research. Educational situations are too complex to fall easily under this principle or that, or to be anticipated in every detail. Moreover, not every detail of the researcher's work can be checked. There is a need for the researcher to be trusted – and thus to be trustworthy.

The moral virtues would be those concerned with the resistance to the blandishments or attractions that tempt one from the research, even where the intellectual virtues press one to go on: courage to proceed when the research is tough or unpopular; honesty when the consequences of telling the truth are uncomfortable; concern for the well-being of those who are being researched and who, if treated insensitively, might suffer harm; modesty about the merits of the research and its conclusions; humility in the face of justified criticism and the readiness to take such criticisms seriously.

This can be illustrated in the importance attached to 'trust'. Clear cases of betrayal of trust are where a promise is broken. There is, of course, something peculiar about the *obligation* to keep promises. Where that obligation is not recognized, the very meaning of 'making a promise' disintegrates. Little value can be attached to promises where it is understood that the promises can be broken when convenient. Keeping promises would seem to be a prima facie duty or principle. However, the trust that is built up between researcher and researched, on the basis of which information is given and intelligence gained, is rarely made explicit in actual promises. It is more a matter of implicit trusting with information, putting oneself in a vulnerable position. This respect for others as vulnerable puts real constraints upon the sensitive evaluator or researcher, however much public importance he or she attaches to the information that has been obtained. It is not possible to say what should be done without examination of the particular case. But the virtuous researcher will be aware of difficulties that others would not be; such a researcher would bring factors into the deliberations that others would omit.

Intellectual virtues would refer to concern to search for the truth and not to cook the books, openness to criticism, an interest in clarity of communication, a concern for evidence. Truth is not always kind and the rewards for its pursuit may be small. Self-interest might suggest cutting corners or being economic with the truth. But genuine researchers would feel ill-at-ease with such behaviours. They would go against the deep-down *feeling* concerning how they ought to act.

The deliberations, therefore, which are inevitable in the complexity of practical situations and the clash of principles that I have spoken of, will be greatly determined by the dispositions or virtues of the researcher. Indeed, even 'telling the truth' might be twisted to a partisan cause if one does not have the right virtues. Was it not William Blake who observed 'A truth that's told with bad intent is worth all the lies you can invent'? The point is that clever people, knowing the conclusions they want, can, if so disposed (i.e. in the absence of the appropriate virtues), find the data and the arguments to justify those conclusions – and yet, despite the fact that no untruth has been told, be dishonest. Research, therefore, as has been argued, requires very special sorts of virtue, both moral and intellectual.

The virtuous research community

Virtues are fostered and, indeed, related to particular social contexts; without that social support, personal virtues so often weaken. A military society will foster a sense of chivalry and honour, and thus the dispositions to act in particular ways. Humility is a distinctively Christian virtue (though too infrequently observed) requiring an institutional support. Kohlberg (1982) came to realize that, without 'just communities', the fostering of the capacity to reason about justice would not translate into dispositions to act justly. Therefore, if we want virtuous researchers, then we must have 'virtuous research communities', communities that embody the very virtues that one requires of the members of those communities.

What, then, are the virtues to be fostered in such communities, which can, in turn, nurture the virtues of their members? Research is primarily concerned with the search for knowledge and the elimination of error. That, in turn, requires the spirit of criticism. Given the tentativeness and provisional nature of most conclusions (for example, that literacy is best improved through the literacy hour or that standards are best improved through naming and shaming), then criticism should be welcomed rather than discouraged. But that goes against the grain. Our natural tendency is to defend rather than criticize our most cherished views. Knowledge might grow through criticism, but knowledge often remains fairly static because the acceptance of such criticism goes against one's natural inclination. Hence, the importance of nurturing in researchers the spirit of self-criticism and the openness to the criticism of others. A research community – in schools, in universities and elsewhere – would provide the forum or the context in which such criticism would be invited and welcomed and become part of the normal life of the institution. But such an invitation is risky. It could open up a range of criticism difficult to sustain. Therefore, the embodiment of such intellectual virtues within the life of a community requires the moral virtue of courage.

But more needs to be said about the community's values in relation to the nature of knowledge claims. The third example, which I gave at the beginning, pointed to the need for negotiation of the research procedures and indeed of its findings. This presupposes a particular respect for the teachers in the school – their distinctive perspective, their insights into the situation, their critical appraisal of the provisional findings. Such respect, reflected in the negotiation of procedures and outcomes, implies a more democratic approach to the conduct of research, an approach based on certain principles but requiring shared dispositions if it is to be carried out. And it is quite clear that few institutions have such 'dispositions', especially when educational programmes are increasingly directed to ends that are external to the deliberations of those communities and have not had to withstand scrutiny within them. By saying the institutions do not have such 'dispositions', I mean that they have not incorporated those norms which influence their members to behave in certain ways. Increasingly, for example, the management of universities excludes the corporate or collegial deliberations over academic aims and values; few schools provide the forum in which teachers might question the educational priorities so often determined by pressures from outside the school. Democratic values (and the social and personal virtues which are associated with them) are difficult to sustain where policy and practice are increasingly controlled by government.

Conclusion

There has been much criticism recently of educational research. Such criticism has focused upon the fragmentation of that research, the irrelevance of that research to the questions which teachers and policy makers are asking, the tendentiousness of some research and the poor quality of the methods adopted. But these criticisms do not address what are possibly the most important questions – namely, those concerned with the qualities (in particular, the virtues) of those carrying out the research. Is there a disposition to find out and to tell the truth as it is and not as one would like it to be? Is there respect for the schools and teachers who are the objects of the research? Have researchers got the courage to resist the opposition of powerful persons when the conclusions are critical? Have they the modesty to recognize the tentativeness of their conclusions? Are they sufficiently trustworthy for us to accept both the data and the conclusions drawn from those data? Furthermore, are they members of a community in which such virtues are respected and fostered – are they allowed to fail?

In beginning to spell out the virtues, I come to recognize my own vices: a salutary experience which others might try!

Note

1 'Club bouncers' are persons employed by night clubs to expel persons who are causing trouble; such trouble includes illegal drug trafficking and violent behaviour.

References

Calvey, D. (2000) Getting on the door and staying there: a covert participant observational study of bouncers, in G. Lee-Treweek and S. Linkogle (eds) *Danger in the Field: Risk and Ethics in Social Research*. London: Routledge.

Kohlberg, L. (1982) Recent work in moral education, in L.O. Ward (ed.) *The Ethical Dimension of the School Curriculum*. Swansea: Pineridge Press.

Mill, J.S. ([1859] 1972) On liberty, in M. Warnock (ed.) *Utilitarianism*. London: Collins.

5 | Against objectivism: the reality of the social fiction

Pierre Bourdieu

Prefatory note to the selection from Pierre Bourdieu

In 2001, Professor Bourdieu was approached and asked to contribute to this collection. The reason for this was that he had made so signal a contribution to an important predecessor book, similarly considering the state of educational research. In 1972, *Knowledge and Control* was given point and direction by two classical papers: one by Basil Bernstein and the second by Pierre Bourdieu.

Anxious to take a similar lead at the present time, the editors requested a contribution to which Professor Bourdieu, by then in ill health, responded by suggesting that extracts be taken from his most recent statement of his intellectual and methodological concerns, *Pascalian Meditations*, which Polity Press published in English in 2000.

Accordingly, Fred Inglis effected the selection from that book which appears in this collection of essays. This is intended to illustrate, in Bourdieu's necessarily abstract, difficult, but always serene prose, his 'twofold truth': that social inquiry is constituted as scientific by virtue of a detachment that may be described as 'objective', but in which objectivism as a doctrine is stoutly repudiated in favour of the fundamental recognition that, in a phrase from these excerpts, 'the social world is an object of knowledge for those who belong to it'. It follows that social science must give 'due place to the efforts of agents to construct their subjective representation of themselves and the world'. This, as Bourdieu acknowledges, entails a sympathetic incorporation of the fact that people devise their own 'sound truths', often in spite of the data.

Thus, the subject and object-matter of Bourdieu's form of enquiry is, in his phrase, 'the economy of symbolic exchange', and in this his name sits easily with that of Clifford Geertz, elsewhere invoked in these pages as doyen of our common inquiries. Bourdieu has, however, a polemical insistence missing from Geertz: his abiding concern is to register the predominant preoccupation of the political left throughout the twentieth century. This is to declare solidarity with human maiming. Consequently, he devises his key concepts of 'symbolic capital' and 'the habitus' to study what seems to him the central mystery of modern society, the allocation of status and the management of ignorance. The habitus is that realm of the social being of each of us within which our knowledge of the past is matched to our assorted dispositions in such a way as to control anticipation and face disappointment. Our symbolic capital is Bourdieu's name for those accumulated resources provided by our class, our history and our experience such that we can invest it, with or without hope, in the mysteries of the future. As Bourdieu himself says in these pages and with some austerity, 'this practical sense of the forthcoming has nothing in common with a rational calculation of chances'. This dictum demands of the human scientist that he or she not only identifies the symbolic expression of social structure in everyday conduct, but discovers within such a symbolization as keen a sense as possible of the matter-of-fact anguish with which people hope for the best and prepare for the worst.

By these processes, individuals accommodate themselves in time; doing so, they learn by way of the non-conscious practices of habitus how few of their social chances (opportunity in the cant) are subjugated to chance itself. Here, as everywhere in his work, Bourdieu insists on the unchanced contribution of the unyielding structures of education to making sure just how very limited opportunity will remain. Social structure tames chance.

This is to make clear with a vengence that social method cannot escape moral commitment. It must either be emancipatory (as in Bourdieu) or managerial (which is to say, the stooge of power). It is, as Bourdieu bleakly points out, only too rare for university enquiry not to fall upon its subordinated knees. 'The dominated are always more resigned than the populist mystique believes', and this is as true of optimistic recipients of ESRC grants as it is of the wretches in the underclass. In this latter connection, he also notes 'the law of the conservation of violence', and looks out grimly for its fulfilment in the corridors of the schools of the poor. The only freedom, by his tokens, is to document the factuality of the social fiction; that is to say, to invest our symbolic capital in alternative fictions that may reduce human brutality and the sentences of insignificance. Either way, his concluding blasphemy might be taken as the maxim of this collection.

I

One cannot remain satisfied with the objectivist vision, which leads to physicalism, and for which there is a social world in itself, to be treated as a thing, with the scientist being able to treat the necessarily partial (in both senses) points of the view of the agents as simple illusions. Nor can one be satisfied with the subjectivist or marginalist vision, for which the social world is merely the product of the aggregation of all representations and all wills. Social science cannot be reduced to an objectification incapable of giving its due place to the effort of agents to construct their subjective representation of themselves and the world, sometimes against all the objective data; and it cannot be reduced to a recording of spontaneous sociologies and folk theories – which are already too present in scientific discourse, smuggling themselves in.

In fact, the social world is an object of knowledge for those who belong to it and who, comprehended within it, comprehend it, and produce it, but from the point of view they occupy within it. One therefore cannot exclude the knowing and the being-known, the recognizing and the being-recognized, which are the source of the struggles for recognition, and for symbolic power, that is, the power to impose the principles of division, knowledge and recognition. But nor can one ignore the fact that, in these truly political struggles to modify the world by modifying the representations of the world, the agents take up positions which, far from being interchangeable, as phenomenist perspectivism would have it, always depend, in reality, on their position in the social world of which they are the product but which they help to produce.

Since one cannot be content either with the primary vision or with the vision to which the work of objectification gives access, one can only strive to *hold together*, so as to integrate them, both the point of view of the agents who are caught up in the object and the point of view on this point of view which the work of analysis enables one to reach by relating position-takings to the positions from which they are taken. No doubt because the epistemological break always presupposes a social separation which, especially when it is ignored, can inspire a form of initiate's contempt for common knowledge, treated as an obstacle to be destroyed and not as an object to be understood, there is a strong temptation – and many social scientists fall into it – to stop short at the objectivist phase and the partial view of the 'half-learned' who, carried away by the wicked pleasure of disenchanting, fail to bring into their analysis the primary vision, Pascal's 'sound truth of the people', against which their constructions are built. The result is that the resistances that scientific objectification often provokes, which are felt and expressed with particular intensity in academic worlds, anxious to defend the monopoly of their own understanding, are not all or always entirely unjustified.

Social games are *in any case* very difficult to describe in their twofold truth. Those who are caught up in them have little interest in seeing the game objectified and those who are not are often ill-placed to experience and feel everything that can only be learned and understood when one takes part in the game – so that their descriptions, which fail to evoke the enchanted experience of the believer, are likely to strike the participants as both trivial and sacrilegious. The 'half-learned', eager to demystify and denounce, do not realize that those they seek to disabuse, or unmask, both know and resist the truth they claim to reveal. They cannot understand, or take into account, the games of self-deception which make it possible to perpetuate an illusion for oneself and to safeguard a bearable form of 'subjective truth' in the face of calls to reality and to realism, and often with the complicity of the institution (the latter – the university, for example, for all its love of classifications and hierarchies – always offers compensatory satisfactions and consolation prizes that tend to blur the perception and evaluation of self and others).

But the defences that individuals put up against the discovery of their truth are as nothing beside the collective systems of defence used to mask the most fundamental mechanisms of the social order, those that govern the economy of symbolic exchanges. Thus the most indisputable discoveries, such as the existence of a strong correlation between social origin and academic success or between level of education and visits to museums, or between gender and the probability of access to the most prestigious positions in the scientific and artistic universes, may be rejected as scandalous untruths to be countered with examples presented as irrefutable ('my *concierge*'s son is at university', or 'I know children of *polytechniciens* who are total failures') or denials which surface, like Freudian slips, in distinguished conversation or in essays aspiring to some seriousness, and the canonical form of which was supplied by a senior member of the most distinguished bourgoisie: 'Education, sir, is innate'. In as much as his work of objectifying and unveiling often leads him to produce the *negation of a denegation*, the sociologist must expect to see his discoveries both swept aside as trivial observations that have been known for all eternity, and violently contested, by the same people, as notorious errors with no other basis than polemical malevolence or envious resentment.

When this has been said, he must not use these resistances, which are very similar to those encountered in psychoanalysis, though more powerful because they are supported by collective mechanisms, as a reason for forgetting that the work of repression and the more or less fantastical constructions that it produces are part of the truth, with the same status as what they seek to disguise. If one recalls, as Husserl does, that 'the arche-original earth does not move', this is not an invitation to repudiate the work of Copernicus in order simply to replace it with the directly experienced truth (as is done by some ethnomethodologists and other constructivist advocates of 'sociologies of freedom', immediately applauded by all those who pine for the 'return of the subject' and the eagerly awaited end of the 'social' and the social sciences). It is simply an invitation to hold together the findings of objectification and the equally clear fact of primary experience which, by definition, excludes objectification. More precisely, it is a question of accepting the permanent obligation of doing what is necessary in order to objectify the scholastic point of view, which enables the objectifying subject to take a point of view on the point of view of the agents engaged in practice, and to adopt a strange point of view, absolutely inaccessible within practice: the dual, bifocal point of view which, having reappropriated its experience as an empirical 'subject', comprehended in the world and also capable of comprehending the fact of implication and all that is implicit within it, endeavours to include in the (inevitably scholastic) theoretical reconstruction the truth of those who have neither the interest nor the leisure nor the necessary instrument to reappropriate the objective and subjective truth of what they are and what they do.

II

Habitus is that presence of the past in the present which makes possible the presence in the present of the forthcoming. It follows from this first that, having within itself its own logic (*lex*) and its own dynamic (*vis*), it is not mechanically subjected to an external causality and that it gives a freedom with respect to direct and immediate determination by the present circumstances (in contrast to what is asserted by mechanistic instantaneism). The autonomy with respect to the immediate event, a trigger rather than a determinant, that is given by habitus (and which becomes manifest when a fortuitous and insignificant stimulus, such as the 'heather-mixture stocking' in *To the Lighthouse*, provokes a disproportionate reaction[1]) is correlative with the dependence on the past that it introduces and which orients one towards a certain forthcoming habitus combines in a single aim a past and a forthcoming neither of which is posited as such. The already-present forthcoming can be read in the present only on the basis of a past that is itself never aimed at as such (habitus as incorporated acquisition being a presence of the past – or to the past – and not memory of the past).

The capacity to anticipate and to see in advance that is acquired in and through practice and familiarization with a field is nothing like a knowledge that can be mobilized at will by means of an act of memory. It is only manifested in concrete situations and is linked as if by a relation of *mutual prompting* to the occasion which calls it forth and which it causes to exist as an opportunity to be seized (whereas someone else would let it pass, unnoticed). Interest takes the form of an encounter with the objectivity of things 'full of interest'. 'We are', says Pascal, 'full of things which take us out of ourselves. Our instinct makes us feel that we must seek our happiness outside ourselves. Our passions impel us outside, even when no objects present themselves to excite them. External objects tempt us of themselves, and call to us, even when we are not thinking of them. And thus philosophers have said in vain: "Retire within yourselves, you will find your good there". We do not believe them, and those who believe them are the most empty and the most foolish'.[2] The things to do, things to be done which are the correlate of practical knowledge, are defined in the relationship between the structure of the hopes or expectations constitutive of a habitus and the structure of probabilities which is constitutive of a social space. This means that the objective probabilities are determinate only for an agent endowed with the sense of the game in the form of the capacity to anticipate the forthcoming of the game. (This anticipation relies on a practical precategorization based on the implementation of the schemes of habitus which, arising from experience of the regularities of existence, structure the contingencies of life in terms of previous experience and make it possible to anticipate in practice the probable futures previously classified as good or bad, bringing satisfactions or frustrations. This practical sense of the forthcoming has nothing in common with a rational calculation of chances – as shown by the discrepancies between an explicit appreciation of probabilities and practical anticipation, which is both more precise and more rapid, as is shown by the experience, familiar to all of us, of the unexpected feeling that occurs when a lift, instead of going straight down to the ground floor, stops at the first floor, when someone has called it, showing us that we have an embodied measurement of the usual duration of the ride, a measurement which cannot be precisely expressed in seconds although it is very accurate, since the gap between the first floor and the ground floor is only a couple of seconds.)

The sense of the game is that sense of the forthcoming of the game, of what is to be done ('it was the only thing to do' or 'he did what was needed') in order to bring about the forthcoming state of the game that is visible there for a habitus predisposed to anticipate it, the sense of the history of the game, which is only acquired through experience of the game – which means that the imminence and pre-eminence of the forthcoming presuppose a disposition which is the product of the past. Strategies oriented by the sense of the game are practical anticipations of the immanent tendencies of the field, never stated in the form of explicit forecasts, still less in the form of norms or rules of behaviour – especially in fields in which the most effective strategies are the ones which appear as the most disinterested. The game, which both provokes and presupposes investment in the game, interest in the game, produces the forthcoming for someone who has something to expect from the game. Conversely, investment or interest, which presupposes possession of a habitus and a capital capable of providing it with at least a minimum of profits, is what brings people into the game, and into the time that is specific to it, that is to say, the forthcoming and the urgencies that it offers. It is proportionate to capital as profit potential – disappearing when the chances of appropriation fall below a certain threshold.

So it is in and by practice, through the practical implication that it implies, that social agents temporalize themselves. But they can 'make' time only in so far as they are endowed with habitus adjusted to the field, that is, to the sense of the game (or of investment), understood as a capacity to anticipate, in the practical mode, forthcomings (*des à venir*) that present themselves in the very structure of the game; or, in other words, in so far as they have been constituted in such a way that they are disposed to see objective potentialities in the present structure which force themselves upon them as things to be done. Time is indeed, as Kant maintained, the product of an act of construction, but it is the work not of the thinking consciousness but of the dispositions and practice.

III

The social world is not a game of chance, a discontinuous series of perfectly independent events, like the spins of a roulette wheel (whose attraction, as Dostoevsky suggests in *The Gambler*, is explained by the fact that it can enable a person to move in an instant from the lowest to the highest rung of the social ladder). Those who talk of equality of opportunity forget that social games – the economic game, but also the cultural games (the religious field, the juridical field, the philosophical field, etc.) are not 'fair games'. Without being, strictly speaking, rigged, the competition resembles a handicap race that has lasted for generations or games in which each player has the positive or negative score of all those who have preceded him, that is, the cumulated scores of all his ancestors. And they should rather be compared to games in which the players progressively accumulate positive or negative profits, and therefore a more or less great capital which, together with the tendencies (to prudence, daring, etc.) inherent in their habitus and partly linked to the volume of their capital, orient their playing strategies.

The social world has a history and, for this reason, it is the site of an internal dynamic, independent of the consciousness and will of the players, a kind of *conatus* linked to the existence of mechanisms which tend to reproduce the structure of the objective probabilities or, more precisely, the structure of the distribution of capital and of the corresponding chances of profit. To speak of a tendency or a *conatus* is to say that, like Popper, one regards the values taken by probability functions as measures of the strength of the propensity of the corresponding events to produce themselves – what Leibniz called their *pretentio ad existendum*. That is why, to designate the temporal logic of this social cosmos, one could speak of the 'order of successions': thanks to the double meaning of the word 'succession', Leibniz's definition of time also evokes the logic of social reproduction, the regularities and rules of the transmission of powers and privileges which is the condition of the permanence of the social order as a regular distribution of *lusiones*, of probabilities or objective expectations.

What determines this redundancy of the social world and, by limiting the space of possibles, makes it livable, capable of being practically foreseen through the practical induction of habitus? On the one hand, there are the tendencies immanent in agents in the form of habitus that are (mostly) coherent and (relatively) constant (over time) and (more or less precisely) orchestrated, which tend (statistically) to reconstitute the structures of which they are the product; and on the other hand there are the tendencies immanent in the social universes, particularly in the fields, which are the product of mechanisms independent of consciousnesses and wills, or of rules or codes explicitly designed to ensure the conservation of the established order (precapitalist societies depend mainly on habitus for their reproduction whereas capitalist societies depend principally on objective mechanisms, such as those which tend to guarantee the reproduction of economic capital and cultural capital, to which should be added all the forms of organizational constraints – one thinks of the postman discussed by Schutz[3] – and codifications of practices, customs, conventions, law, some of which are expressly designed, as Weber observes, to ensure predictability and calculability).

IV

I have so far argued as if the two dimensions constitutive of temporal experience – subjective expectations and the objective chances, or more precisely the actual or potential power over the immanent tendencies of the social world which governs the chances attached to an agent (or his or her position) – were identical for all; as if, in other words, all agents had both the same chances of material and symbolic profit (and were therefore, in a sense, dealing with the same economic and social world) and the same dispositions to invest. But agents have powers (defined by the volume and structure of their capital) which are very unequal. As for their expectations and aspirations, these are also very unequally distributed (despite some cases of mismatch with the capacities for satisfaction), by virtue of the law that, through the dispositions of habitus (themselves adjusted, most of the time, to agents' positions) expectations tend universally to be roughly adapted to the objective chances.

This tendential law of human behaviours, whereby the subjective hope of profit tends to be adjusted to the objective probability of profit, governs the propensity to invest (money, work, time, emotion, etc.) in the various fields. So it is that the propensity of families and children to invest in education (which is itself one of the major factors of educational success) depends on the degree to which they depend on the educational system for the reproduction of their capital and their social position, and on the chances of success for these investments in view of the volume of the cultural capital they possess – these two factors combining to determine the considerable differences in attitudes towards schooling and in success at school (those for example which separate the child of a university teacher from the child of a manual worker, or even the child of a primary teacher from the child of a small shopkeeper).

One is always surprised to see how much people's wills adjust to their possibilities, their desires in the capacity to satisfy them; and to discover that, contrary to all received ideas, *pleonexia*, the desire always to have more, as Plato called it, is the exception. This is true even in societies where, with the generalization of schooling, generating a structural *déclassement* linked to the devaluation of educational qualifications, and the generalization of insecurity of employment, the mismatch between expectations and chances becomes more frequent. Whenever the dispositions that produce them are themselves the product of conditions identical or similar to those in which they are implemented, the strategies that agents use to defend their actual or potential position in social space and, more generally, their image of themselves – always mediated by others – are objectively adjusted to these conditions – which does not mean that they necessarily correspond to the interests of their authors. For example, the realistic, even resigned or fatalistic, dispositions which lead members of the dominated classes to put up with objective conditions that would be judged intolerable or revolting by agents otherwise disposed can have the appearances of purposiveness only if it is forgotten that, by a paradoxical counterfinality of adaptation to reality, they help to reproduce the conditions of oppression.

Thus power (that is, capital, social energy) governs the potentialities objectively offered to each player, her possibilities and impossibilities, her degrees of empowerment, of power-to-be, and at the same time her desire for power, which, being fundamentally realistic, is roughly adjusted to the agent's actual empowerment. Early and lasting insertion into a condition defined by a particular degree of power tends, through experience of the possibilities offered or denied by that condition, to institute durably in the body dispositions-to-be which are (tendentially) proportioned to these potentialities. Habitus is this 'can-be' which tends to produce practices objectively adjusted to the possibilities, in particular by orienting the perception and evaluation of the possibilities inscribed in the present situation.

To understand the realism of this adjustment, one has to take account of the fact that the automatic effects of the conditionings imposed by the conditions of existence are added to by the directly educative interventions of the family, the peer group and the agents of the educational system (assessments, advice, injunctions, recommendations), which expressly aim to favour the adjustment of aspirations to objective chances, needs to possibilities, the anticipation and acceptance of the limits, both visible and invisible, explicit and tacit. By discouraging aspirations oriented to unattainable goals, which are thereby defined as illegitimate pretensions, these calls to order tend to underline or anticipate the sanctions of necessity and to orientate aspirations towards more realistic goals, more compatible with the chances inscribed in the position occupied. The principle of all moral education is thus set out: become what you are (and what you have to be) socially, do what you have to do, what is incumbent upon you – this is Plato's *ta autou prattein* – an 'ought to be' which may require a supersession of self ('noblesse oblige') or recall one to the limits of what is reasonable ('that's not for you').

V

Thus, social scientists regularly forget the economic and social conditions which make possible the ordinary order of practices, in particular those of the social world. Now, there exists, in the social world, a category, that of the subproletarians, which highlights these conditions by showing what happens when life is turned into a 'game of chance' (*qmar*), as an unemployed Algerian put it, and when the limited desire for power which is habitus in a sense capitulates before the more or less long-lasting experience of powerlessness. Just as, as psychologists have observed, the annihilation of chances associated with crisis situations leads to the collapse of psychological defences, so here it leads to a kind of generalized and lasting disorganization of behaviour and thought linked to the disappearance of any coherent vision of the future. Thus, better than any 'imaginary variations', this analyser requires one to break with the self-evidences of the ordinary order by bringing to light the presuppositions tacitly engaged in the view of the world (which are common to phenomenological analysis and the theorization of rational action theory or Bayesianism).

The often disorganized and even incoherent behaviours, constantly contradicted by their discourse, of these people without a future, living at the mercy of what each day brings and condemned to oscillate between fantasy and surrender, between flight into the imaginary and fatalistic surrender to the verdicts of the given, are evidence that, below a certain threshold of objective chances, the strategic disposition itself, which presupposes practical reference to a forthcoming, sometimes a very remote one, as in the case of family planning, cannot be constituted. The real ambition to control the future (and, *a fortiori*, the project of conceiving and rationally pursuing what the theory of rational anticipations calls 'subjective expected utility') varies with the real power to control that future, which means first of all having a grasp on the present itself. It follows that, far from contradicting the law of correspondence between structures and habitus, or between positions and dispositions, the dream-like ambitions and millenarian hopes that the most deprived sometimes express still testify that, in contrast to this imaginary demand, real demand has its basis and therefore also its limits in real power. When listening to subproletarians – unemployed Algerians in the 1960s or adolescents living without prospects on desolate housing estates in the 1990s – one discovers how the powerlessness that, by destroying potentialities, prevents investment in social stakes engenders illusions. The link between the present and the future seems to be broken, as is shown by the projects they entertain, completely detached from the present and immediately belied by it: sending a daughter to university when it turns out that she has already abandoned school, or setting up a leisure centre in the Far East when there is no money for travelling anywhere.[4]

In losing their work, the unemployed have also lost the countless tokens of a socially known and recognized *function*, in other words the whole set of goals posited in advance, independently of any conscious project, in the form of demands and commitments – 'important' meetings, cheques to post, invoices to draw up – and the whole forthcoming already given in the immediate present, in the form of deadlines, dates and timetables to be observed – buses to take, rates to maintain, targets to meet . . . Deprived of this objective universe of incitements and indications which orientate and stimulate action and, through it, social life, they can only experience the free time that is left to them as dead time, purposeless and meaningless. If time seems to be annihilated, this is because employment is the support, if not the source, of most interests, expectations, demands, hopes and investments in the present, and also in the future or the past that it implies, in short one of the major foundations of *illusio* in the sense of involvement in the game of life, in the present, the primordial investment which – as traditional wisdom has always taught, in identifying detachment from time with detachment from the world – creates time and indeed *is* time itself.

Excluded from the game, dispossessed of the vital illusion of having a function or a mission, of having to be or do something, these people may, in order to escape from the non-time of a life in which nothing happens and where there is nothing to expect, and in order to feel they exist, resort to activities which, like all the lotteries or gambling systems of all the world, offer an escape from the negated time of a life without justification or possible investment, by recreating the temporal vector and reintroducing expectation, for a moment, until the end of the game or Sunday night, in other words finalized time, which is in itself a source of satisfaction. And, to try to escape from the sense, so well expressed by the Algerian subproletarians, of being the plaything of external constraints ('I'm like a scrap of peel on water'), and to break out from a fatalistic submission to the forces of the world, the younger of them especially may also use acts of violence which in themselves count for more than, or as much as, the profits they procure, or death-defying games with cars or motorbikes, as a desperate way of existing in the eyes of others, for others, of achieving a recognized form of social existence or, quite simply, of making something happen rather than nothing.

Thus, the limiting-case experience of those who, like the subproletarians, are excluded from the ordinary (economic) world has the virtues of a kind of radical doubt: it forces one to raise the question of the economic and social conditions which make possible access to time as something so self-evident as to pass unnoticed. It is indeed certain that the scholastic experience which in its very principle involves a very particular relation to time, based on a fundamental freedom with respect to the ordinary logic of action, in no way aids understanding of different experiences of the world and of time, or understanding of itself, especially as regards temporality.

The extreme dispossession of the subproletarian – whether of working age or still in that ill-defined zone between schooling and unemployment or underemployment in which many working-class adolescents are kept, often for a rather long time – brings to light the self-evidence of the relationship between time and power, by showing that the practical relation to the forthcoming, in which the experience of time is generated, depends on power and the objective chances it opens. It can be confirmed statistically that investment in the forthcoming of the game presupposes a basic minimum of chances in the game, and therefore power over the game, over the present of the game; and that the aptitude to adjust behaviour in relation to the future is closely dependent on the effective chances of controlling the future that are inscribed in the present conditions. In short, adaptation to the tacit demands of the economic cosmos is only accessible to those who possess a certain minimum of economic and cultural capital, that is, a certain degree of power over the mechanisms that have to be mastered. It is all the more necessary to make this point because, in addition to the effect of the scholastic condition which, like gravity, affects everything we think without becoming visible, there is the specific effect of public time. Being defined in mathematical or physical terms, this astronomical time is naturalized, dehistoricized, desocialized, becoming something external which flows 'of itself and by its nature' as Newton put it, and which thus helps to conceal the links between power and the possible under the appearances of the consensus that it helps to produce.

VI

The 'causality of the probable' which tends to favour the adjustment of expectations to chances is no doubt one of the most powerful factors of conservation of the established order. On the one hand, it ensures the unconditional submission of the dominated to the established order that is implied in the doxic relation to the world, an immediate adherence which puts the most intolerable conditions of existence (from the point of view of a habitus constituted in other conditions) beyond questioning and challenge. On the other hand, it favours the acquisition of dispositions which, being adjusted to disadvantaged, declining positions, threatened with disappearance or overtaken by events, leave agents ill-prepared to face the demands of the social order, especially inasmuch as they encourage various forms of self-exploitation (I am thinking in particular of the sacrifices undertaken by the clerical workers or junior executives who have taken on enormous debts so as to become home-owners).[5]

The dominated are always more resigned than the populist mystique believes and even than might be suggested by simple observation of their conditions of existence – and above all by the organized expression of their demands, mediated by political and trade union spokespersons. Having adapted to the demands of the world which has made them what they are, they take for granted the greater part of their existence. Moreover, because even the harshest established order provides some advantages of order that are not lightly sacrificed, indignation, revolt and transgressions (in starting a strike, for example) are always difficult and painful and almost always extremely costly, both materially and psychologically.

And this is true, despite appearances, even of adolescents, who might be thought to be radically at odds with the social order, to judge from their attitude to their 'elders', whether at home, at school or in the factory.[6] Thus, while he rightly emphasizes the acts of resistance, often anarchic and close to delinquency, with which working-class adolescents fight against schooling, and also against their 'elders', and through them against working-class traditions and values, Paul Willis also describes the rigidity of this harsh world, dedicated to the cult of toughness and virility (women only exist there through men, and recognize their own subordination).[7] He shows clearly how this cult of male strength, the extreme form of which is the exaltation of 'lads' (another focus of populist mythology, especially as regards language), is based on the affirmation of a solid, stable, constant world, collectively guaranteed – by the gang or the group – and, above all, profoundly rooted in its own self-evidences and aggressiveness towards anything different. As is shown by a profoundly rigid mode of speech, which refuses abstraction in favour of the concrete and of common sense, emotionally supported and punctuated by striking images, *ad hominem* appeals and dramatizing expletives, and also by a whole ritual – stereotyped terms of address, nicknames, mock fights, nudging, etc. – this world-view is profoundly conformist, especially on points as essential as everything concerned with social hierarchies, and not only between the sexes. Revolt, when it is expressed, stops short at the limits of the immediate universe and, failing to go beyond insubordination, bravado in the face of authority or insults, it targets persons rather than structures.[8]

In order not to naturalize dispositions, one has to relate these durable ways of being (I am thinking for example of 'plain speaking' or the – very moving – gruffness of moments of intense emotion) to the conditions of their acquisition. Habitus of necessity operate as a defence mechanism against necessity, which tends, paradoxically, to escape the rigours of necessity by anticipating it and so contributing to its efficacy. Being the product of a learning process imposed by the sanctions or injunctions of a social order acting also as a moral order, these profoundly realist dispositions (close sometimes to fatalism) tend to reduce the dissonances between expectations and outcomes by performing a more or less total closure of horizons. Resignation is indeed the commonest effect of that form of 'learning by doing' which is the teaching performed by the order of things itself, in the unmediated encounter with social nature (particularly in the form of the sanctions of the educational market and the labour market), next to which the intentional actions of domestication performed by all the 'ideological State apparatuses' are of little weight.

And the populist illusion which is nowadays nourished by a simplistic rhetoric of 'resistance' tends to conceal one of the most tragic effects of the condition of the dominated – the inclination to violence that is engendered by early and constant exposure to violence. There is a *law of the conservation of violence*, and all medical, sociological and psychological research shows that ill-treatment in childhood (in particular, beatings by parents) is significantly linked to increased chances of using violence against others in turn (often one's own companions in misfortune), through crime, sexual abuse and other forms of aggression, and also on oneself, especially through alcoholism and drug addiction. That is why, if we really want to reduce these forms of visible and visibly reprehensible violence, there is no other way than to reduce the overall quantity of violence which is neither noticed nor punished, the violence exerted every day in families, factories, workshops, banks, offices, police stations, prisons, even hospitals and schools, and which is, in the last analysis, the product of the 'inert violence' of economic structures and social mechanisms relayed by the active violence of people. The effects of symbolic violence, in particular that exerted against stigmatized populations, do not tend, as the lovers of humanist pastorals seem to believe, always to favour the emergence of successful realizations of the human ideal – even if, to stand up against the degradation imposed by degrading conditions, agents always find some defences, individual or collective, momentary or durable, being durably inscribed in habitus, such as irony, humour or what Alf Lüdtke calls *Eigensinn*, 'stubborn obstinacy', and so many other misunderstood forms of resistance.[9] (This is what makes it so difficult to talk about the dominated in an accurate and realistic way without seeming either to crush them or exalt them, especially in the eyes of all the do-gooders who will be led by a disappointment or a surprise proportionate to their ignorance to see condemnations or celebrations in informed attempts to describe things as they are.)

VII

Through the social games it offers, the social world provides something more and other than the apparent stakes: the chase, Pascal reminds us, counts as much as, if not more than, the quarry, and there is a happiness in activity which exceeds the visible profits – wage, prize or reward – and which consists in the fact of emerging from indifference (or depression), being occupied, projected towards goals, and feeling oneself objectively, and therefore subjectively, endowed with a social mission. To be expected, solicited, overwhelmed with obligations and commitments is not only to be snatched from solitude or insignificance, but also to experience, in the most continuous and concrete way, the feeling of counting for others, being *important* for them, and therefore in oneself, and finding in the permanent plebiscite of testimonies of interest – requests, expectation, invitations – a kind of continuous justification for existing.

One of the most unequal of all distributions and probably, in any case, the most cruel, is the distribution of symbolic capital, that is, of social importance and of reasons for living. And it is known, for example, that even the treatment and care that hospital institutions and agents give to the dying are varied, more unconsciously than consciously, according to their social importance.[10] In the hierarchy of worth and unworthiness, which can never be perfectly superimposed on the hierarchy of wealth and powers, the nobleman, in his traditional variant, or in his modern form – what I call the State nobility – is opposed to the stigmatized pariah who, like the Jew in Kafka's time or, now, the black in the ghetto or the Arab or Turk in the working-class suburbs of European cities, bears the curse of a negative symbolic capital. All the manifestations of social recognition which make up symbolic capital, all the forms of perceived being which make up a social being that is known, 'visible', famous, admired, invited, loved, etc., are so many manifestations of the grace (*charisma*) which saves those it touches from the distress of an existence without justification and which gives them not only a 'theodicy of their own privilege', as Max Weber said of religion – which is in itself not negligible – but also a theodicy of their existence.

Conversely, there is no worse dispossession, no worse privation, perhaps, than that of the losers in the symbolic struggle for recognition, for access to a socially recognized social being, in a word, to humanity. This struggle is not reducible to a Goffmanian battle to present a favourable representation of oneself: it is competition for a power than can only be won from others competing for the same power, a power over others that derives its existence from others, from their perception and appreciation, and therefore a power over a desire for power and over the object of this desire. Although it is the product of subjective acts of donation of meaning (not necessarily implying consciousness and representation), this symbolic power, charm, seduction, charisma, appears endowed with an objective reality, as if determining the gazes which produce it (like *fides* as described by Emile Benveniste or charisma as analysed by Max Weber, himself a victim of the effects of fetishization both of the transcendence arising from the aggregation of gazes and above all of the concordance of objective structures and incorporated structures).

Every kind of capital (economic, cultural, social) tends (to different degrees) to function as symbolic capital (so that it might be better to speak, in rigorous terms, of the *symbolic effects of capital*) when it obtains an explicit or practical recognition, that of a habitus structured according to the very structures of the space in which it has been engendered. In other words, symbolic capital (male honour in Mediterranean societies, the honourability of the *notable* or the Chinese mandarin, the prestige of the celebrated writer, etc.) is not a particular kind of capital but what every kind of capital becomes when it is misrecognized as capital, that is, as force, a power or capacity for (actual or potential) exploitation and therefore recognized as legitimate. More precisely, capital exists and acts as symbolic capital (securing profits – as observed, for example, in the maxim 'honesty is the best policy') in its relationship with a habitus predisposed to perceive it as a sign, and as a sign of importance, that is, to know and recognize it on the basis of cognitive structures able and inclined to grant it recognition because they are attuned to what it is. Produced by the transfiguration of a power relation into a sense relation, symbolic capital rescues agents from insignificance, the absence of importance and of meaning.

To be known and recognized also means possessing the power to recognize, to consecrate, to state, with success, what merits being known and recognized and, more generally, to say what is, or rather what is to be thought about what is, through a performative act of speech (or prediction) capable of making what is spoken of conform to what is spoken of it (a power of which the bureaucratic variant is the legal act and the charismatic variant is the prophetic pronouncement). Rites of institution, acts of symbolic investiture intended to justify the consecrated being in being what it is, existing as it exists, literally *make* the person to whom they are applied by raising him or her from illegal exercise, the delirious fiction of the imposter or the arbitrary imposition of the usurper. This it does by declaring publicly that he is indeed what he claims to be, that he is legitimated to be what he claims, that he is entitled to enter into the function, fiction or imposture which, being proclaimed before the eyes of all as deserving to be universally recognized, becomes a 'legitimate imposture' in Austin's phrase, in other words *misrecognized*, denied as an imposture by all, not least by the imposter himself.

In solemnly imposing the name or title which defines him in an inaugural ceremony of enthronement – the *inceptio* of a medieval master, the ordination of a priest, the dubbing of a knight, the crowning of a king, an inaugural lecture, the opening session of a court, etc., or, in a quite different order of things, circumcision or marriage – these acts of performative magic both enable and require the recipient to become what he is, that is, what he has to be, to enter, body and soul, into his function, in other words into his *social fiction*, to take on the social image or essence that is conferred on him in the form of names, titles, degrees, posts or honours, and to incarnate it as a legal person, the ordinary or extraordinary member of a group, which he also helps to make exist by giving it an exemplary incarnation.

Rites of institution give an enlarged and particularly visible image of the effect of the institution, an arbitrary being which has the power to rescue from arbitrariness, to confer the supreme *raison d'être*, the one constituted by the affirmation that a contingent being, vulnerable to sickness, infirmity and death, is worthy of the dignity, transcendent and immortal, like the social order, that he is given. And acts of nomination, from the most trivial acts of bureaucracy, like the issuing of an identity card, or a sickness or disablement certificate, to the most solemn, which consecrate nobilities, lead, in a kind of infinite regress, to that realization of God on earth, the State, which guarantees, in the last resort, the infinite series of acts of authority certifying by delegation the validity of the certificates of legitimate existence (as a sick or handicapped person, an *agrégé* or a priest). And sociology thus leads to a kind of theology of the last instance: invested, like Kafka's court, with an absolute power of truth-telling and creative perception, the State, like the divine *intuitus originarius* according to Kant, brings into existence by naming and distinguishing. Durkheim was, it can be seen, not so naive as is claimed when he said, as Kafka might have, that 'society is God'.

Notes

1 Woolf, V. (1927) *To the Lighthouse*. London: Hogarth Press; and Auerbach, E. (1953) Mimesis: The Representation of Reality in Western Literature, pp. 525ff. Princeton, NJ: Princeton University Press.
2 Pascal, *Pensées*, 464.
3 Schutz, A. (1962) *Collective Papers*, Vol. 2, p. 45. The Hague: Martinus Nijhoff.
4 Bourdieu, P. (1964) *Travail et travailleurs en Algérie*, pp. 352–62. Paris: Mouton; Bourdieu, P. (1993) *La Misère du monde*, pp. 607–11. Paris: Editions de Minuit [translated in Bourdieu, P. (1999) Those were the days, in *The Weight of the World*. Cambridge: Polity Press].
5 cf. Bourdieu, P. *et al.* (1990) L'économie de la maison, *Actes de la Recherche en Sciences Sociales*, No. 81–2 (March).
6 Pialoux, M. (1979) Jeunes sans avenir et travail intérimaire, *Actes de la Recherche en Sciences Sociales*, No. 26–7, pp. 19–47.
7 Willis, P.E. (1978) *Profane Culture*. London: Routledge & Kegan Paul; and

Willis, P.E. (1977) *Learning to Labour: How Working Class Kids get Working Class Jobs*. Aldershot: Ashgate.

8 Among the subproletarians of Algeria, I observed the same inclination to denounce or condemn persons rather than institutions or mechanisms.

9 Ludtke, A. (1996) Ouvriers, *Eigensinn* et politique dans l'Allemagne du Xxe siècle, *Actes de la Recherche en Sciences Sociales*, No.113 (March), pp. 91–101.

10 cf. Glaser, B.G. and Strauss, A. (1965) *Awareness of Dying*. Chicago, IL: Aldine; and Glaser, B.G. and Strauss, A. (1968) *Time for Dying*. Chicago, IL: Aldine.

6 | Research as thoughtful practice

Jon Nixon, Melanie Walker and Peter Clough

> Without the breath of life the human body is a corpse; without thinking the human mind is dead.
>
> (Arendt 1978, Vol. 1: 123)

We take as our starting point the relation between thought, action and judgement as explored by Hannah Arendt throughout her life but particularly in her later work. Arendt defines the purpose of human thought with reference to the structural features of human agency. Thinking, she argues, is the means by which all human beings grapple and come to terms with the boundless indeterminacy of action. Thinking can never have an instrumental, means/end relation to action precisely because (a) the consequences of any action are indeterminate and (b) the prime purpose of thought is to seek to understand that indeterminacy. Thinking 'is not a prerogative of the few but an ever-present faculty in everybody; by the same token, inability to think is not a failing of the many who lack brain power, but an ever-present possibility for everybody' (Arendt 1978, Vol. 1: 191). We locate Arendt's elaboration of the relation between thought, action and judgement within a broader Aristotelian frame of reference, in which we seek to position the practice of educational research.

This conceptualization of the relation between thought, action and judgement does not lend itself well to prevailing trends within educational research. We live in an evidence-sodden society: that for which there is no evidence is beyond cognizance. We have lost the nerve for bold inductive inferences that project beyond the known data. Yet that is precisely what thought requires. Policy makers whose policies were entirely and exclusively evidence-based would be incapable of projecting into an unknown and uncertain future. Similarly, practitioners whose practice was entirely and exclusively evidence-based would be incapable of foresight and circumspection. This is not to say that evidence is irrelevant to thinking, but to emphasize that its relevance must be understood. Research exists not only to provide policy makers and practitioners with evidence, but to provide as a public resource interpretations of that evidence that speak to the conditions pertaining at precise points and within specific public sectors.

Evidence itself is neither good nor bad. The crucial questions are: What is deemed to be evidence? Who deems it relevant or otherwise? From whom and by whom is it gathered? And by what means? To what ends is it used? And by whom? These are not technical questions; they involve moral considerations and require moral deliberation. In claiming that they are significant methodological questions, we are making the further claim that methodology (the study of method) must itself be morally grounded. For us, that moral ground requires an approach to educational research that recognizes the commonality of thought and that engages the public in thoughtful debate regarding the ends and purposes of education.

What is required, then, to restore thoughtfulness to the field of educational research is neither a rejection of the important traditions of empirical data gathering, nor a refusal to engage with the practical import of scholastic endeavour. Both these refusals would represent a retreat into some latter-day ivory tower. What is required, rather, is an insistence on educational research as integral to an inclusive tradition of thoughtful public deliberation, which acknowledges the unpredictability of human action and the primacy of human agency; an insistence, that is, on research as common resource. The purpose of this chapter is to assert the public role of educational research through a definition of research as thoughtful practice.

Thought and action

Thinking has increasingly become the preserve of the professional thinker. Since the Enlightenment, that preserve has become increasingly bounded by the institutional contexts and tribal divides of intellectual workers. Within the second half of the twentieth century, the balance of power within and across those institutional contexts shifted significantly between the academy, the publishing houses and the media (see Debray 1981; Bourdieu 1998). Arguably, it was the academy that lost out in that battle for the heritage of thought (particularly, perhaps, in the UK during the years of Thatcher government). It is now columnists in major papers, pundits on networked news programmes and a handful of public intellectuals that manage to achieve bestseller status who are seen as the purveyors of thought. Academics fall into these various categories, but it is not primarily through the academy that they achieve their voice: it is through newspapers, television and major publishing houses. Thinking remains the preserve of the few, but the few are more variously assembled. A striking feature of the recent history of educational publishing in particular is the demise of a 'general' readership (see Nixon 1999).

That breaking down of institutional boundaries, and with it the crumbling of the mythical ivory tower, is no bad thing. However, it leaves the academy in a defensive and vulnerable position and it leaves the mass of academics marginalized from the competing pluralistic contest of public opinions, the *doxai*, which is their lifeblood. It has also created a new elite of those who have access to the new institutions of public thought and those who can only read and listen and occasionally bang on the doors of public opinion. The academy must find a new sense of purposefulness, a *telos*, if it is to square up to its historic mission; and academics, stratified and diversified as never before, have a key role to play in this process of intellectual reconstruction (see Nixon 2001a; Walker 2001a).

Thought gains its legitimacy from the structure of action: multiple agents acting in an agonistic, or tragic, world of human affairs within which action is theoretically boundless, and irreversible, in its largely unforeseeable consequences (see Nixon 2001b). Because the values underlying action are incommensurable and because in the playing out of action in a plural world contingency is always a key factor, conflict and unpredictability are part of the ground plan. 'The great tragic plots', argues Nussbaum,

> explore the gap between our goodness and our good living, between what we are (our character, intentions, aspirations, values) and how humanly well we manage to live. They show us reversals happening to good-charactered but not divine or invulnerable people, exploring the many ways in which being of a certain good human character falls short of sufficiency for *eudaimonia* ('human flourishing').
>
> (Nussbaum 1986: 382)

Thinking is the way in which human beings make sense of, and seek to learn from, such reversals, so as to maximize the possibility of 'human flourishing'. 'There is a gap', as Williams (1993) puts it, 'between what the tragic character is, concretely and contingently, and the ways in which the world acts upon him' (pp. 164–6). Thinking is the means by which we seek to render that gap comprehensible. It is our response to the tragic structure of human life. Thinking is rooted in, and must be re-routed towards, the human capacity for recognizing and making sense of the implications of multiple agency. The possibility of agency is what distinguishes the tragic or agonistic world view from fatalistic and providential world views. Destiny, within the agonistic frame, is the agent's life work. 'The modern person', writes Heller (1990: 6) 'is born as a cluster of possibilities without telos . . . [and] it must choose the framework, the telos, of his or her life' (quoted in Plummer 2001: 263).

MacIntyre makes a similar point when he argues that

> Unpredictability and teleology . . . coexist as part of our lives; like characters in a fictional narrative we do not know what will happen next, but nonetheless our lives have a certain form which projects itself towards our future. Thus the narratives which we live out have both an unpredictable and a partially teleological character.
>
> (MacIntyre 1985: 216)

The thinking agent, then, is not merely determined by unpredictable events, but can shape and determine the outcome of events through purposeful action. To 'stop and think', as Arendt put it, is the only way human beings have of forestalling the unthinking acquiescence to the onward rush of events. The 'banality of evil', as Arendt (1965) controversially perceived it in Eichmann, lay in his, and others', 'absence of thinking'. ('It was unthinkable that I would not follow orders', wrote Eichmann.) Therein lay the roots of totalitarianism. When the chips are down it is only this capacity, and will, to 'stop and think' that can save us from calamity.

Thought's inherent gesture is that of reaching out: to the other in oneself and the various others that make up this world of difference. Arendt (1968a) characterized this mode of thought as 'representative thinking', because in 'the dialogue of the two in one who I am' (the self) may be represented the thought of various and possibly conflicting voices (the other). 'Representative thinking' is the human capacity, which (although given) requires development and encouragement, to 'think from the standpoint of somebody else'. To become thoughtful, each of us must, in Arendt's (1968b) phrase, learn 'to think without banisters' (*Denken ohne Gelander*), to climb the stairs without the security of known categories; because, for each, the other is different, and the challenge of the other unique. Thinking is a moral necessity, without which right action is unthinkable and the onward rush of events irreversible. The only alternative to thoughtfulness (as envisaged by Arendt) is the thoughtlessness of solipsism and its political counterparts: totalitarianism, despotism and the politics of violence.

The world is an increasingly dangerous and unpredictable place: insecure and risky as never before (Beck 1999). It is 'a fluid and unpredictable world of deregulation, flexibility, competitiveness and endemic uncertainty' (Bauman 2001: 144). Risks no longer simply accumulate but, according to Beck and Bauman, constitute our social space. We can neither deny nor collapse into the radical instability that constitutes this world and that increasingly threatens to engulf it. We must grow up and, in growing up, grow into a renewed thoughtfulness regarding our responsibility towards the future of a world seriously at risk. Shouldering that responsibility requires the virtues of truthfulness, courage and obedience regarding the futures beyond our own life-spans. It also requires a civil society, comprising institutional frameworks and social structures, to sustain and nurture those virtues. The university, conceived as a place of thoughtful practice, should be a cornerstone of that civil society.

The question, for those of us with a specific concern for educational research, is how the university (especially, perhaps, those universities designated as 'civic') can rise to that challenge: how research conducted in the interests of, and on behalf of, education can become more cognizant of its moral duty to nurture thought within and throughout the *polis*. In addressing that question, we are aware that intellectual workers like ourselves have a fight on their hands. But we are also aware that, as Bourdieu (1996: 348) put it, 'the fight must be *collective* because the effectiveness of the powers which are exercised over them results in large part from the fact that those intellectuals who confront them are dispersed and in competition with each other'. As Bourdieu argues, 'criticism and watchfulness' are required, but these must be both inward and outward looking: towards a critical engagement with both our own research practice and the world through which that practice gains its sense of purposefulness.

If we are to take seriously the notion of the boundlessness of human action as developed by Arendt, educational settings cannot be understood in isolation or even in relation to one another. They must be seen, and studied, as inescapably implicated in the wider social and political order. Similarly, if we are to take seriously her notion of the irreversibility of human action, what we seek to understand can only be understood over time. It must be seen, and studied, as part of the temporal order subject to contingency and unforeseen circumstance. Finally, if human agency as understood by Arendt is to be taken seriously, then educational processes cannot be reduced to, or understood in terms of, 'educational outcomes'. The latter cannot be pre-specified.

To achieve thoughtfulness, then, educational research must not only broaden its scope, but also extend its reach in terms of the constituencies with which it seeks to engage. This raises issues that are too often marginalized in the current debate on research methodology. Who decides which are the important questions for which we need to produce and collect evidence? Whose questions get asked and answered? Whose problems are investigated? What indeed counts as evidence and whose evidence (or voice) counts? Evidence-based policy and practice offer no inherent guarantee that they will benefit communities or inflect towards thoughtful deliberation. Indeed, they may equally inflect away from thoughtful deliberation by privileging outcomes and ends at the expense of processes and purposes. In so doing, they not only limit the scope for debate, but also render it mindless.

How, then, are diverse publics to participate in thoughtful educational research? We are reminded here of Spivak's (1995) pivotal question: 'Can the subaltern speak? – when the subaltern speaks back to the colonizing power, she asks, whose worldview is actually being spoken?' Attempts to generate inclusion in South Africa, for example, in the early 1990s through the National Education Policy Commission were revealing of how voice and participation through participatory policy research in unequal contexts of power and skill are both deeply important and deeply problematic. A reflexive, 'academic' social science becomes arguably even more pivotal (for details of this South African example, see Muller 2000). At issue is how we *do* participation in the spaces between thought and action in ways that take us closer to ideals of thoughtful research. How do we realize practices of public deliberation without putting scholarship at the explicit service of politics? How do we produce better (more thoughtful) research and better (more trustworthy) knowledge (see Walker 2001b)?

The practice of thoughtful research

To explore these questions, we offer 'readings' of three instances of what we take to be thoughtful research. They are deliberately very different from each other, although they have some things in common. The point is that we wish to exercise care in offering these examples so that we hold open the debate about what thoughtful research might look like in action. It would seem contrary to the idea of thoughtful research to claim with certainty that 'this is what and how it is'. Such thinking leads us into the sterile dead end of checklists for 'effective' practice and the limited approach of method- or technique-led research, both of which we vehemently eschew.

Tentatively, then, we think the examples that follow have these things in common, and having these things in common they begin to point to how we might name thoughtful research. Crucially, they are historically and contextually located and framed. They are examples of the reiterative and reflexive re-reading of texts and stories, both those we produce ourselves and those texts and stories produced by others. Central to this reading is a disposition to critique and analysis, and a dialectic that comprises both theorizing and the working and re-working of the data or evidence we have to hand. Thus evidence counts, but it is always embedded in analytical processes and open to review and reinterpretation. In different ways, each of the examples offers a view on research relationships shaped by difference, whether the differences are between those in the academy and those outside, whether they are differences of status, subject disciplines, social class, gender, race or occupation.

Our three examples, again in their different ways, are moral and ethical projects that take as central to social inquiry our individual and collective responsibilities for the human condition. This is reflected in the research questions asked, in the research processes by which answers are sought, and in the analytical and interpretive processes through which the evidence is understood and explained.

In different ways, too, each project seeks to deal creatively and positively with difference, not as something to be overcome, but as contributing positively to the research and practice process and the quality of the research knowledge produced. Conditions of dialogue are established that allow diverse perspectives and opinions to be voiced. All three projects demonstrate in different ways scholarship-in-action in the world, whether through the practical attempts to improve student learning, through the attempt to develop a practical feminist politics, or in attempts to bring everyday life to the attention of policy makers and politicians. In all cases, scholarship is seen to inform practical and public deliberations of different kinds and in diverse settings.

Thoughtful research I

The first example, which we suggest approaches our ideal of 'thoughtful' research, involved one of us. Melanie Walker collaborated over two years with a group of five lecturers from different disciplines at the University of Glasgow, an ancient Scottish university. This work was written up and published as an edited text, *Reconstructing Professionalism in University Teaching: Teachers and Learners in Action* (Walker 2001a). Against a contextual framing of changing conditions of higher education, the group worked together to reconstruct their own professionalism in university teaching through a collaborative and reflexive professional dialogue regarding the ends and purposes of learning, explored in discipline-based educational action research projects. Despite current uncertain and risky times, the drive in higher education teaching and learning is towards prediction, control and certainties. Action research, they thought, would be one way to prise open these claims to certainty about the way the (educational) world is in pursuit of better educational practices, not tips or checklists. They worked to open the space from which to 'talk back' to the marketization of higher education, to assert critical agency for themselves and their students, and to reclaim the wisdom and complexity of their own professional judgements. Through layered processes of professional dialogue and learning, and classroom research and student learning, they worked to rebuild professional identities (who we are in higher education) more consistent with their educational values of collegiality, collaboration and equity. While the shifts that resulted might have only been small accretions of local change, the broader purpose was still for equity in learning and society. The point was not just to talk about, or theorize about, but to *do* a critical professionalism in their teaching and learning practices in higher education. At stake were practices of 'criticality', which encouraged students not only to learn about their world and learn about themselves, but to develop themselves and act in the world.

The group assumed that their practical experiences in education were open to reflection, reworking and critique within a democratic knowledge-making project. The process involved action, participation, improvement, collaboration, inclusion and critical self-reflection. Crucially, their action research studies also involved other epistemological communities – their students, and their thoughts and concerns. A 'banking' process between full vessels and empty receivers would have been as inappropriate in their research as in their teaching. Student experiences and their voices counted in the creation and legitimization of knowledge about education and learning. But for this group, action research was also consistent with the kind of pedagogical principles that they espoused – where students are agents of their own knowing, and agents in the construction of knowledge about curriculum, teaching and learning. Everyone has a stake in developing pedagogical knowledge. On the other hand, involving students was not uncomplicated; it worked patchily in practice. When power 'speaks' in particular ways in higher education pedagogy, it is not surprising that students are unsure: Is it a kind of hidden assessment? Is it really about their best interests?

Central to constructing a new professionalism in university teaching, and to working as teachers and learners in action, were their processes of collaboration and a double dialectic of both personal development and critical community. At the same time, this project shows that collaboration is not inherently liberatory; much turns on the context and practices that give it form and no one trajectory defines all collaborations. Thus what we also learn from this project, given the aspirations of 'thoughtful research' to be inclusive of diverse communities, is that spaces of collaboration are unpredictable and complex as the 'ideas and actions of one person interact with the ideas and actions of another to produce a co-construction' (Griffiths 1998: 13). Yet therein also lies their richness and possibility. It is at the knotty points and moments of disagreement and unpredictability that we gain insights into each other and ourselves and generate the spaces and intersections that are simultaneously uncomfortable and yet satisfying and productive. Indeed, friction kept them open to the challenges posed to their own thinking, even though the rasp of disagreement and difference were hard and difficult in practice. There were important epistemological aspects to their collaboration as well. If hegemony works to perpetuate the *status quo* and maintain control, then keeping open different ways of seeing and voicing different experiences seems significant if we are to avoid consensual relations (or a search for them) hardening into their own hegemonic regime of truth within a group. Obliterating disagreements and eliminating frictions may well simply mask the power relations which are anyway present in any interactive encounter. Thus consensus and agreement may well be more rather than less problematic.

At issue is that working with many different voices and different perspectives in a framework of mutual support and knowledge generates more responsible and inclusive knowledge. Collaboration is, then, also ethically desirable. In the case of this project, this was (and is) very unlike dominant modes of knowledge production in the academy that are competitive and adversarial (even where working in 'teams' is part of the process). For this group, then, critical collaboration was a way of being as well as a way of thinking, a challenge to dominant discourses of professionalism and a market in higher education, and a way to enrich and expand their practice of research.

In this project, then, we see the importance of the policy and social context and the way it influences our practices of, and judgements about, teaching and research. At the same time we have agency, which enabled this group to search out the spaces for a different way of being in higher education. Generating educational knowledge through research was central and this process involved practical experiences, gathering evidence and also the analytical dialogue that each lecturer deployed individually and through collaborative dialogue to challenge their own assumptions about learning. At issue was how to describe and explain educational action. Such knowledge was generated through the involvement of the lecturers in researching their own teaching, rather than being the objects of research by others, and then in disseminating work to colleagues and finding ways to influence teaching and learning policy in the university. In other words, they sought continually to expand the 'public' sphere of dialogue, participation and influence.

Thoughtful research II

The second example to which we wish to point is Bourdieu and co-workers' (1999) *The Weight of the World: Social Suffering in Contemporary Society*. Although not strictly speaking educational research, we believe its methodology and substantive concerns to be deeply relevant to the study of education. This text details the work over three years undertaken by Bourdieu and a team of sociologists who set out to document the new forms of social suffering that characterize contemporary societies. When it was originally published in France in 1993, the book topped the bestseller lists and stimulated wide-ranging public debates on inequality, civic solidarity and politics. The research team's concern was indeed to bring the lives of ordinary men and women, with few means to make themselves heard, to the attention of politicians and state officials.

The project, detailed in over 600 pages, was to describe and understand new forms of suffering produced in declining housing estates, the school, the family, street-level state services, the everyday world of social workers and policemen, among factory workers and white-collar clerks, the world of farmers and artisans, of teachers and the unemployed and partly employed. The stories recounted are fascinating, moving and compelling.

They include the family from the former French colony of Algeria, now living on a housing estate outside Paris where they have to cope with pervasive continuing racism; the story of a steelworker laid off after 20 years in the same factory and now struggling to support his family on unemployment benefits; the story of a schoolteacher trying to cope with deteriorating urban teaching conditions and the lack of 'intelligent' relationships between teachers and students; the story of a representative of the youth wing of the extreme right; the story of a woman, part of a generation and milieu which assumed that wives stayed at home and who experienced feminism only as an adult; the story of the trade unionist who finds his goals undermined by the changing nature of work; and the disabled woman determinedly struggling to go beyond her physical limitations, while constantly being reminded of these limits by everyone around her.

At one level the accounts offered might be read as 'short stories', perspectives on contemporary life and suffering as experienced by people from diverse walks of life in a relatively materially privileged country. At issue is what Bourdieu calls 'positional suffering', in which he challenges platitudes that take as their point of reference the (privileged) macrocosm and those retorts such as: 'You really don't have anything to complain about' or 'You could be worse off, you know'. Bourdieu goes on to explain that using material poverty as the sole measure of suffering 'keeps us from seeing and understanding a whole side of the suffering characteristic of a social order which, although it has undoubtedly reduced poverty (though less than is often claimed) has also multiplied the social spaces (specialized field and sub-fields) and set up the conditions for an unprecedented development of all kinds of ordinary suffering' (p. 4).

In collecting, through interviews, and then publishing these stories, the methodology of narrative and analysis was central; the text comprises stories and methodological discussions and theoretical analyses. The methodological challenge in making very private worlds public was both to anonymize actual identities and to protect informants as far as possible from being misrepresented. To this end, Bourdieu quotes Spinoza's maxim: 'Do not deplore, do not laugh, do not hate, understand'. A theoretical narrative works to offer readers the means of this understanding, which, says Bourdieu, 'means taking people as they are' but also 'providing the theoretical instruments that let us see these lives as necessary through a systematic search for the causes and reasons they have for being what they are' (p. 1). The breadth and inclusiveness of the evidence and analysis works to challenge 'commonsense' of the variety in which people 'too clever by half' claim on the slenderest of evidence (a schoolgirl wearing a headscarf) to know what is going on in the social world, what Bourdieu scathingly calls the 'science of little learning that opinion polls are' (p. 620). Thus the text has a dual thrust of narrative and causes that works to undermine individual pathologies by excavating the social basis of suffering, 'of unhappiness in all its forms, including the most intimate, the most secret' (p. 629).

Key to the researchers' approach were principles of respect, openness and attentiveness to the subtle ways in which people make sense of their own lives. Bourdieu attempts to make explicit the intentions and procedural principles the team employed to enable readers to see how the work of production and understanding was undertaken. His interest is a research practice that is 'reflective and methodical' (p. 608), disciplined by an awareness of the work of construction. At stake is trying to reduce as much as possible the symbolic violence that characterizes research relationships so that informants are not turned into research objects. While they try mentally to put themselves in the place of their informants, at the same time the researchers do not claim to cancel the social distance between themselves as researchers and their informants. What is aspired to is a 'welcoming disposition, which leads one to make the respondent's problems one's own, the capacity to take that person and understand them just as they are in their distinctive necessity' (p. 614), which Bourdieu describes as a kind of 'intellectual love' (p. 614). The researcher's craft is 'a disposition to pursue truth', which says Bourdieu 'disposes one to improvise on the spot, in the urgency of the interview, strategies of self-presentation and adaptive responses, encouragement and opportune questions, etc., so as to help respondents deliver up their truth or, rather, to be delivered of it' (p. 621).

Importantly, these stories of suffering are not cause for despair in Bourdieu's view. On the contrary, understanding how the social world works provides the means, the knowledge, to work towards undoing it through 'the margin of manoeuvre left to liberty, that is, to political action' (p. 629). Thus 'thought', 'judgement' and 'action' (however minimal) must be braided together as thoughtful research works to expose contradictions and produce awareness of how the world is.

Thoughtful research III

Finally, as our third example, we suggest that Jean Barr's (1999) text *Liberating Knowledge: Research, Feminism and Adult Education* similarly approaches what we are grasping towards understanding as 'thoughtful' research. *Liberating Knowledge* offers a reflexive account of Barr's experiences in adult education, feminist theory and practice, and research in various settings over a period of fifteen years. She discusses three cases of her own research, all broadly in the field of women's education. The first involved an evaluation of a pre-school community education project in Glasgow, as part of a national study of alternative forms of pre-school provision in 1979–81. Her second research project was a study conducted in 1989–90 for a masters dissertation in which she explored the influence of different forms of feminism on New Opportunities for Women courses in the North of England. Her third was a funded research project from 1991 to 1993 on 'Women's perceptions of science' in the adult education curriculum.

Her research practices demonstrate her own enduring concern with the 'democratic control and development of knowledge' as 'an ideal of citizenship' (p. 191), and hence with education, research and social practices where power and culture intersect with real material effects for people's lives. Adopting an autobiographical approach that acknowledges the richness of our 'storied lives', she nonetheless recognizes that personal experience as a source of knowledge is not some kind of 'trump card of authenticity' (p. 4). Indeed, Barr is careful to point out that our understandings are open to reworking and to critique, and that other voices, including theoretical resources, are key to being personal *and* critical. In other words, she has in mind not some form of narcissistic self-review but a public dialogue. Moreover, the self also changes and develops over time – the reflexive self assembled by Barr in this book is not quite the same as the selves that undertook each of the research projects. Her critical scrutiny includes her own practices and judgements developed in and from the space between thought and action; it is not aimed primarily or only at others. Thus her process of re-view and reappraisal of what her research 'masks as well as reveals, for its blindspots as well as its illuminations' (p. 4), demonstrates practically her belief that we need to cultivate greater self-understanding, even though such self-knowledge is itself always provisional and open to further reworking.

As important as her self-critical scrutiny is the way in which she locates her research in particular social contexts and historical moments. Threaded through these accounts is the story of the culturally and historically specific forms that feminism took in the UK in the 1970s, the 1980s and into the 1990s. In each case, she provides extracts from the original research reports and then critiques the silences and gaps. In the case of the pre-school research project, her Marxist-feminist theoretical categories are now seen to have excluded whatever 'escaped' these categories, for example women's caring work and the 'small transgressions' and resistances by working-class women. In her second project, still 'seduced by theory with a capital T' (p. 156), she veered uncomfortably close to a 'banking' view of feminist education in which tutors deposit expert theoretical knowledge in the heads of their students. In the third study, however, a more reflexive personal voice 'was allowed in' and there was not the same attempt as in her previous two research projects to fit what women said into pre-determined categories of the researchers. Eschewing, then, a narrow view of reflexivity, she locates this work within a wider social and historical context of knowledge production, shaped by the prevailing discourses, power relations and material conditions.

There is much to be gained epistemologically, methodologically and, indeed, pedagogically from this book for those of us committed both to an ideal of thoughtful research and the 'scholastic attitude', and to research as a common resource. As Barr points out, the democratic knowledge-making project, resonant with complexity and values, is currently under siege from a technicist (thoughtless) discourse and practices that position student and pupil 'consumers' as the recipients of knowledge for purely instrumental ends. Education (including schooling, higher and adult) is increasingly being seen as a private asset rather than a public good, so that we risk erasure of the underlying educational purposes that give educational and institutional practices a particular kind of meaning for learners and teachers. Barr explicitly raises the importance of articulating 'urgent problem with people other than academics' (p. 163). She seeks to heal the breach between 'words' (ideas, discourses, academic knowledge) and 'things' (material conditions, everyday experiences). As she explains, 'knowledge contained in books is limited if it is not connected to people's aspirations for knowledge about how to live in the world' (p. 163). Barr urges those privileged to have time for research and theorizing 'to leave the internal debates of the academy' (p. 163). In her view, being overly deferential to academic knowledge 'all too often goes hand in hand with a failure to produce really useful knowledge, that is, knowledge which enables an understanding of human experience, enhances self-respect and helps people to deal critically and creatively with the world in order to change it' (p. 163). It means enabling 'subjugated knowledges' to be heard and listened to in enlarged and inclusive conversations.

At the same time, this returns us to Spivak's question. Moreover, Barr's text itself demonstrates the difficulties and ambiguities of this commitment both to scholarship and the inclusion of many voices. She cites Lorraine Code, who points out the complexity of struggles to hear and be heard (p. 16). Barr herself has produced a fine and compelling text of her own reassembling of the self and of 'responsible knowledge', and she has taken care to review the experiences and voices of women in her earlier research. But while she aligns herself with those who believe that we can develop better self-understanding of our social world through more 'democratic knowledge-making practices and structures' (p. 9), her own text, deftly and elegantly woven though it is, is also resonant with difficult theoretical ideas, as any education masters students not familiar with this language might point out.

Yet this same calm analytical narrative is indispensable to her text and to her methodology. Eder (1999: 209) asks the hard question: 'Why is it so difficult to change the world? The answer would be: because societies don't like to learn. They would rather stick to what they know and to the rules that stabilise what they know' (quoted in Muller 2000: 137). The point is that a metanarrative of critical theorizing is, we suggest, central to a thoughtful research practice, to the possibility of generating emancipatory insights and to developing critical resources for participatory approaches and a common resource. Participation in research and public deliberation as a goal or ideal and participation and deliberation as an assumption of equality are, then, not the same thing. As Muller (2000: 141) reminds us: ' "equality" and "empowerment" as desired social ends, will be fatally stymied if we do not have ways of understanding how our very social arrangements . . . collude with the *status quo* in ways that are not immediately evident to common sense'. The point is the non-transparency of everyday life. He goes on to add: 'The challenge is how to deal dialectically and relationally with systemic issues from the vantage point of the self-understanding of actors' (p. 142); or, put another way, dealing dialectically with structure and agency, thought and action, in order to open up the 'complicity between positions and dispositions' (Bourdieu, 1992: 136).

Democratizing judgement

> we must imagine how a more radically democratised science could help us develop a civic community.
>
> (Brown 1998: 194)

We would argue that the above instances of what we see as thoughtful research are attempts to bridge the gap between thought and action through the exercise of practical research-led judgement and a practical politics in education and social life, what Aristotle termed *phronesis*. Arendt (1968a) viewed judgement as a specifically political ability; the ability, that is, 'to see things not only from one's own point of view but from the perspective of all those who happen to be present' (p. 221). Following Iris Young (2000), such practical judgements provide 'the epistemic conditions for the collective knowledge of which proposals are most likely to promote results which are wise and just' (p. 30), to take us closer to 'public' and responsible deliberations. Arendt elaborates this particular view of judgement as follows:

> The Greeks called this ability [to judge] *phronesis*, or insight, and they considered it the principal virtue or excellence of the statesman in distinction from the wisdom of the philosopher. The difference between this judging insight and speculative thought lies in that the former has its roots in what we usually call common sense, which the latter constantly transcends. Common sense . . . discloses to us the nature of the world insofar as it is a common world; we owe to it the fact that our strictly private and 'subjective' five senses and their sensory data can adjust themselves to a nonsubjective and 'objective' world which we have in common and share with others. Judging is one, if not the most, important activity in which this sharing-the-world-with-others comes to pass.
>
> (Arendt 1968a: 221)

For Arendt, the political (broadly understood) involves a certain sort of relationship both to oneself and others, the chief hallmark of which is the capacity for critical judgement about the society in which we live. The processes through which these critical (thoughtful) capacities are developed is deeply and inescapably social; by communicating across differing experiences and perspectives in a shared (public) space, there is an enlarged understanding of the world through which our educational research might be produced.

Judgement, as 'sharing-the-world-with-others', is necessary because in our diverse and unpredictable social world precise rules of application are impossible, since such applications are dependent on local contexts and 'there are too many contexts to allow for full specification of the possibly relevant rules and how they might be locally applied' (Brown 1998: 63). To the extent that situations are routinized and predictable, they are more amenable to routinized methods of interpretation and analysis. However, social situations rarely manifest regularity and predictability. Therein lies their complexity and the need for 'reasoned judgment that adapts shared principles to changing circumstances . . . The more publicly significant the issue, the less likely it is to be predictable' (Brown 1998: 189).

The issues that educational research addresses are invariably of this order. It is important to know, for example, what the rates of unjustified absenteeism are in particular schools, but this knowledge is of value only in so far as it informs judgement as to why those rates are as they are and how the schools concerned might respond to the problem of unjustified absenteeism. Because judgement requires a consideration of the moral appropriateness of ends and means, it can only be exercised in the context of shared principles, dialogue and with a keen sense of changing circumstances. It requires 'discrimination, discernment, imagination, sympathy, detachment, impartiality, and integrity' (d'Entreves 2000: 245).

Expert knowledge, as Brown argues, is too often silent regarding the moral appropriateness of ends and of the means to achieve those ends:

> Thus expert calculation is a necessary but not a sufficient condition for prudent choice. In addition prudence involves a knowledge of ethical purposes and consequences. It is a substantive type of rationality that seeks the good for human beings and citizens in particular circumstances. Further, because prudence is a moral kind of knowledge, virtue in the knower bolsters prudence with ethical steadfastness and intuition of the good . . . Both virtue and prudence are necessary to make an expert a good human and a good citizen.
>
> (Brown 1998: 220)

Brown's notion of 'a substantive type of rationality' is very close to what we mean by 'thoughtfulness': the capacity to be mindful of the public good in the forming of judgements regarding right action. Neither the a-rational moralism nor the a-moral technicism of much of what passes for 'thought' in contemporary society serves us well in this respect. What is required is the recognition of 'a "public good" or "civic ideal" to which people may appeal in deliberation which transcends specific individual and group interests' (Fuller 2000: 15). In our view, educational research has a major contribution to make to such deliberation.

Conclusion

We conclude, not with a summative statement, but with some pointers and questions that have emerged from, and are grounded in, our earlier 'readings' of specific instances of what we have termed 'thoughtful research' and its relationship to practical judgements that seek to improve our lives in education and society.

The thinking agent-as-researcher

As thinking or thoughtful agents, we acknowledge that we have the ability to make and re-make judgements, albeit constrained by our contextual conditions of possibility. In the wider world, we do have choices as to whether we align ourselves with, or in opposition to, social forces that increase the gap between rich and poor and between North and South. Within education, we do have choices as to whether we speak and act for fairness in education, or against it. Are we for increased knowledge only, or for increased social justice also? This capacity for agency and action requires of us that we act ethically, critically and responsibly in making our research choices and in the doing of that research with others.

Thinking together

Thinking is at once the most isolating and most socializing of our capacities. In advocating thoughtful research we are seeking, therefore, not to deny the necessary solitude of thought, but to relocate it in what Arendt termed 'this world of interdependence':

> Even if I shun all company or am completely isolated while forming an opinion, I am not simply together only with myself in the solitude of philosophical thought; I remain in this world of universal interdependence, where I can make myself the representative of everybody else.
>
> (Arendt 1968a: 242)

We need, then, not only to think, but to recognize that thought is a human necessity. I cannot think for you, and you cannot think for me. Somehow we must learn to think *together*, or cease to exist as humans. There is no alternative. Thoughtfulness requires public engagement and a commitment to participation – to multiple voices, perspectives and experiences. Increasingly, the problems facing society are shared problems (litter, traffic congestion, terrorism, etc.) that can only be addressed by our thinking together and acting together (see Touraine 2000). Our failure to think together, imaginatively and across boundaries, *is* the problem, and in our view it is *the* problem that what we call thoughtful research should seek to address.

Positionality and analytical reflexivity

But thinking together also requires our sensitivity to, rather than an unhelpful erasure of, the power relationships in our research and the production of knowledge that results. In doing our research we are ourselves positioned by virtue of our class, gender, race, sexuality, and so on. Neither we nor the subjects we seek to understand are blank social slates; we are embedded within particular biographies and the communities from whom we take our identities. This requires of us a deep and vigilant reflexivity in our research that is attentive to the effects of our own peripheral vision. We might begin with standpoint experiences and voices – both our own and those of others – but we cannot end there. We must go on to interpose an analytical narrative that seeks to understand, to explain and to theorize how the (educational) world is: what Gramsci (1971) described as fashioning 'good sense' out of 'common-sense'.

What can thoughtful research do?

Doing thoughtful research means accepting that there are limits to what research in/of/for education can do. Precisely because our research takes place within particular social and political formations, its impact will, in turn, be shaped by the ideas and values that prevail. Educational research, like all educational activity, is politically driven and value-saturated. At issue is to keep asking ourselves: 'What can I *do* from where I am?' and 'How can I *do* it in ways that enlarge and enhance the democratic knowledge-making project and public deliberation?' (*Doing* – action, agency – was, for Arendt, the key constituent of politics and of morality.) Our conceptualization of thoughtful research takes up the challenge of both these questions and, in so doing, seeks to give them practical educational life.

These questions and pointers are not, of course, endpoints. Taking as our starting point scattered insights derived from Arendt's reflections upon the relation between thought, action and judgement, we find the beginnings of a different kind of methodological discourse: one grounded in the moral purposefulness of thinking agents engaged in the task of learning how to think together and ever mindful of our radically different positionalities and of the agonistic structuring of this world of human affairs: 'without thinking the human mind is dead'.

References

Arendt, H. (1965) *Eichmann in Jerusalem: A Report on the Banality of Evil*. New York: Viking Press (revised and enlarged edition).

Arendt, H. (1968a) *Between Past and Future: Six Exercises in Political Thought*. New York: Viking Press (revised edition, including two additional essays).

Arendt, H. (1968b) *Men in Dark Times*. New York: Harcourt, Brace & World.

Arendt, H. (1978) *The Life of the Mind*. New York: Harcourt Brace Jovanovich (two volumes of an uncompleted work, published posthumously and edited by Mary McArthy).

Barr, J. (1999) *Liberating Knowledge: Research, Feminism and Adult Education*. Leicester: NIACE.

Bauman, Z. (2001) *Community: Seeking Safety in an Insecure World*. Cambridge: Polity Press.

Beck, U. (1999) *World Risk Society*. Cambridge: Polity Press.

Bourdieu, P. (1992) The practice of reflexive sociology, in P. Bourdieu and L.J.D. Wacquant, *An Invitation to Reflexive Sociology*. Cambridge: Polity Press

Bourdieu, P. (1996) *The Rules of Art: Genesis and Structure of the Literary Field* (trans. S. Emanuel). Cambridge: Polity Press.

Bourdieu, P. (1998) *On Television and Journalism* (trans. P. Parkhurst). London: Pluto Press.

Bourdieu, P. *et al.* (1999) *The Weight of the World: Social Suffering in Contemporary Society* (trans. P. Ferguson). Cambridge: Polity Press.

Brown, R.H. (1998) *Toward a Democratic Science: Scientific Narration and Civic Communication*. New Haven, CT: Yale University Press.

Debray, R. (1981) *Teachers, Writers, Celebrities: The Intellectuals of Modern France*. London: Verso.

D'Entreves, M.P. (2000) Arendt's theory of judgment, in D. Villa (ed.) *The Cambridge Companion to Hannah Arendt*. Cambridge: Cambridge University Press.

Eder, K. (1999) Societies learn and yet the world is hard to change, *European Journal of Social Theory*, 2: 192–215.

Fuller, S. (2000) *The Governance of Science: Ideology and the Future of the Open Society*. Buckingham: Open University Press.

Grasmci, A. (1971) *Selections from the Prison Notebooks*. London: Lawrence & Wishart.

Griffiths, M. (1998) Secrets and lies, communication to the Annual British Educational Research Association conference, Belfast.

Heller, A. (1990) *Philosophy of Morals*. Oxford: Blackwell.

MacIntyre, A. (1985) *After Virtue: A Study in Moral Theory*. London: Duckworth (second corrected edition with postscript).

Muller, J. (2000) *Reclaiming Knowledge: Social Theory, Curriculum and Education Policy*. London: Falmer Press.

Nixon, J. (1999) Teachers, writers, professionals: is there anybody out there?, *British Journal of Sociology of Education*, 20(2): 207–21.

Nixon, J. (2001a) 'Not without dust and heat': the moral bases of the 'new' academic professionalism, *British Journal of Educational Studies*, 49(2): 173–86.

Nixon, J. (2001b) Imagining ourselves into being: conversing with Hannah Arendt, *Pedagogy, Culture and Society*, 9(2): 221–36.

Nussbaum, M. (1986) *The Fragility of Goodness: Luck and Ethics in Greek Tragedy and Philosophy.* Cambridge: Cambridge University Press.

Plummer, K. (2001) *Documents of Life 2: An Invitation to a Critical Humanism.* London: Sage.

Spivak, G. (1995) Can the subaltern speak?, in B. Ashcroft, G. Griffiths and H. Tiffin (eds) *The Post-Colonial Studies Reader*. London: Routledge.

Touraine, A. (2000) *Can We Live Together? Equality and Difference*. Cambridge: Polity Press.

Walker, M. (ed.) (2001a) *Reconstructing Professionalism in University Teaching: Teachers and Learners in Action*. Buckingham: SRHE & Open University Press.

Walker, M. (2001b) Making better knowledge: little stories, truth-telling and social justice effects, *The School Field: An International Journal of Theory and Research in Education*, 12(1/2): 55–68.

Williams, B. (1993) *Shame and Necessity*. Berkeley, CA: University of California Press.

Young, I.M. (2000) *Democracy and Inclusion*. Oxford: Oxford University Press.

7 | On goodness and utility in educational research

Carrie Paechter

Introduction

In recent years – and probably over a much longer period – there have been repeated pronouncements by governments, policy makers and others that focused on the utility, or lack of it, of educational research. These pronouncements appear mainly to have concentrated on complaints that educational researchers are ivory-tower academics who do little that has any relation to the real world and, in any case, if they do, fail to disseminate it properly to 'end users', the (often undefined) people who need it. Tooley and Darby (1998) referred to 'researchers largely doing their research in a vacuum, unnoticed and unheeded by anyone else' (p. 75), while Hillage *et al.* (1998), having described the involvement of practitioners as governed by 'rampant ad hocery' (p. x), went on to propose that,

> mediation needs to be built in at the start of research and we would encourage researchers and research funders to identify strategies for maximising the impact of the research at the outset. In addition, researchers should be encouraged to identify the audiences for their research and the appropriate intermediaries, and target them accordingly.
>
> (Hillage *et al.* 1998: xiv)

There is thus an assumption that there is a group of people who use, or should use, the findings of educational research, and that research should specifically be targeted to service these groups; that is, that educational research should be concentrated in areas where it will be particularly useful and reported in such a way that its utility is obvious.

Against this background, what I want to do here is to ask a number of questions related to these assumptions about the nature of educational research. I want to consider what people mean when they talk about 'educational research'; how this is related to a focus on its utility; what we mean when we talk about research being useful; and what difference it would make if we laid these considerations of utility to one side when considering what constitutes good educational research.

Educational research as an applied discipline

Educational research sees itself, and is seen, as an applied discipline – or at least as the application of several disciplines. This seems to be for a number of reasons. First, there is the expectation of outsiders. It is reasonable, at least on some level, for educational research to be concerned with the practice of education. While accepting this, however, it is important to keep in mind a crucial distinction. Doing research into practice does not directly imply doing research aimed at changing that practice – indeed, much anthropology and sociology is concerned, at least while the research is going on, to leave practice alone. Despite this, though, educational policy makers and practitioners expect that, even if we do not intervene when the research is being carried out, the effects of that research should be some kind of intervention, albeit not necessarily at the level at which the research took place: classroom-based research could lead to policy changes, for example. So educational research is understood by those outside of it, including teachers,[1] as not only being about researching into practice, but also about influencing that practice for the better. If it just adds to knowledge without carrying an explicit and direct message about what to do as a result, they are puzzled.

This way of looking at the field is shared by many educational researchers, including teachers, and seems to be coupled with an assumption that educational research should be – or should mainly be – empirical, and should address specific, answerable questions. This second aspect may be connected with the focus of many commentators on 'value for money' (Hargreaves 1996). Non-empirical research, by and large (for example, work on education history, or scholarly work focusing mainly on ideas rather than on events and processes in practice, or research that might be called 'empirical at a distance', reanalysing existing data sets or bringing together findings from a range of researchers or disciplines) is cheaper and, therefore, more hidden than any of the wide variations in empirical forms that require external funding and whose utility is, as a result, more often called into question (Hargreaves 1996). This emphasis may also be related to the ways in which those providing external funding for research tend to assume that the work will both be empirical and result in new data sets as well as usable and applicable conclusions. I think, however, that this assumption is again related to the way that utility has become closely associated with educational research. It can be difficult to see immediately how non-empirical work can have direct or even indirect application in classrooms and seminars. Those of us whose work could more accurately be described as 'scholarly', bringing ideas from a range of sources to bear on questions that relate to education but that do not have immediate, practical application (such as, in my own case, work on the relationship between gender, power and knowledge),[2] are seen as being even further up the ivory tower than the rest of the educational research community, even more distant from practitioners, producing research that may 'count' in social science disciplines but which is less than central to the work of education, either as a research field or in practice.

Hence, although I would argue that, for example, scholarly analysis has an important place in educational research, the commonly held idea seems to be that it is work that is empirical, based on the practical problems of teachers in classrooms (with less emphasis on other people in other educational settings), and useful in its outcomes. Most educational researchers, including the 'scholars', also share with teachers and with the general public an aspiration that educational research should influence what goes on in classrooms and staffrooms. This is partly because, as human beings, we want to feel that what we do is worthwhile, to convey to others things that interest ourselves, to have an impact on the world. If our research really does change teaching and learning, this impact is obvious and, therefore, rewarding. Many people involved in educational research are also working with practitioners or practitioners-in-training on a day-to-day basis as part of their teaching role. This means that we are constantly reminded of the non-researcher's assumption that what we do must be useful for practice, and are regularly asked to justify our research work in these terms. Finally, many of us ourselves have had previous careers as teachers and retain some of that feeling that educational research is a waste of time if it does not help me in my classroom, if not today, then fairly soon.

There is thus an underlying assumption held by educational researchers, policy makers and the wider public that our research should have some application to practice, and that we should put some effort into ensuring this happens. However, I think we need at least to ask ourselves whether short- or medium-term usefulness really is the most important factor in what constitutes good educational research.

What constitutes good educational research?

In discussing what is meant by educational research, Mortimore notes its enormous range and scope:

> Research ranges from studies of the learning of babies and young children, through to the lifelong learning of the university of the third

> age and of those who learn outside of educational institutions. It includes anything to do with the educative process – formal and informal – and many topics within health, childcare or delinquency. It may focus on places (schools, playgrounds, libraries or homes) or on people (pupils, teachers, childcare workers, support staff, chief education officers or civil servants). Just as medicine tries to deal with health and sickness, causes and effects, prognoses and sequelae, education is concerned with the whole person and their mental, spiritual, physical and emotional developments.
>
> (Mortimore 2000: 11–12)

One of the effects of this wide range is that educational research, as an applied discipline, relates both to the field of education and to its disciplines of origin. Although many educational researchers see themselves straightforwardly as educationalists, others are much more clearly psychologists, sociologists, historians, and so on who happen to work in the field of education. These people may have sound reasons for working within education and may, indeed, have spent all their research lives there, but they retain an outlook and allegiance to these underpinning disciplines and focus their research around them. They may also see their work as contributing to these other disciplines as well as to education: Janus-like, they simultaneously look towards and address the worlds of education and of their disciplinary base. For others, however, this is not the case. Many educational researchers started off studying the disciplines that they then taught in schools, coming to educational research only subsequently. These people may bring the assumptions of these originating disciplines to the work they do in education, but they do not reflect back into them: those people working in science education, for example, while they may retain some science-based assumptions about how research is conducted, do not see themselves as serving the science as well as the science education community (except in terms of keeping up the supply of new scientists). For these two groups of researchers, what constitutes good research may well be shared, but utility will be measured in different ways and with different emphases.

We have, therefore, to see educational research in terms both of contributing to related disciplines and in terms of education itself. The relative weight that is given to each will vary according to the research under consideration, but both aspects will influence whether a particular piece of research is good or not. At the same time, it does seem to be clear that if a piece of research is good, then it is good both in education and in any originating discipline; it doesn't seem to me that it would make sense to say that a piece of research founded in psychology was a good piece of educational research but bad psychology. Thus, in discussing goodness in educational research, I shall assume that goodness within the field of education can be taken to imply goodness from the point of view of any founding discipline to which it is closely related.

So what does constitute goodness in educational research? Partly this is a moral question, and we should not be afraid to identify it as such. In using 'goodness' rather than 'efficiency', 'effectiveness' or 'rigour', for example, I am implying at least that some judgement of moral worth is pertinent to this issue. This is possibly clearer in fields related to education than in education itself. It seems to me that there is some research that simply should not take place, because it is founded in, or has the potential to lead to, differential treatment of human beings. Research underpinned by racist or sexist assumptions about particular groups would fall into this category. Good educational research needs to be related to ends, purposes and intentions that are themselves morally justifiable. A necessary condition for goodness in educational research is thus that it is, at a minimum, founded in explict and morally defensible principles. We then need to examine other factors that influence whether or not it may be considered good. My continued use of this term is intended to underline my understanding that, properly conducted, educational research is a morally constituted endeavour.

Clearly, such research needs to relate to education but, as Mortimore points out above, this has to be very broadly understood. The 2001 UK Research Assessment Exercise (HEFC 2001)[3] gave the following as its definition of what counted as part of the Education Unit of Assessment, again reflecting a very wide brief:

> Pre-school, primary, secondary, further, higher, teacher or other professional, adult, continuing, vocational and community education or training, work-based learning and lifelong learning. Assessment, curriculum, teaching, pedagogy, learning, and information and communication technologies in education. Special educational needs; counselling; comparative, international and development education; education and industry; education policy; organisation, governance and management; social exclusion/inclusion and equity issues in education. History, psychology, philosophy, sociology and other disciplines of education. Qualitative, quantitative, ethnographic, evaluation, action research and other methodological procedures used in educational research.
>
> (HEFC 2001: section 4)

In judging the worth of educational research in an exercise designed to do just that – and in terms of its intrinsic worth as research, not necessarily of its utility – the Research Assessment Exercise education panel had to see education and its research as being both independent and related to constituent and independent disciplines (which, in turn, had their own relatively long definitions). Educational research is a complex beast and is not easy to pin down. The suggestions I give here for judging its goodness will, therefore, inevitably reflect my own biases, and are really only presented as a workable sample: others may have other, more or less related ideas. What I want to emphasize, however, is that we can have notions of what constitutes good educational research, in both the moral and the good-as-properly-conducted senses, that are independent of any judgements about its utility.

First, good educational research is rigorous, in its planning, execution and reporting. Research questions should be clear, or when they cannot be, this itself should be made explicit, for example by openness about the work's exploratory nature. Researchers need to be honest with themselves, as well as with others, about what they have seen, what they have assumed and what they can conclude. This rigour can be difficult to achieve when practitioners and policy makers want results (containing answers) rapidly. Hammersley (1997) notes that 'one important cause of the unsatisfactory nature of much educational research is that it is too preoccupied with producing information that will shape *current* policy or practice' (p. 146, emphasis in original). Such information has to be in a particular form, and often, this form (brief, bullet-pointed, without too many qualifications and counterpositions) does not encourage rigour either in data collection or in its analysis.

Second, and related to this, good research in education and allied fields must be transparent in its methods. This does not, however, imply a principle of replicability. Because educational research concerns itself essentially with human beings and their learning, the researcher cannot always be controlled for in the way he or she can be in the pure sciences. Different researchers may get different responses, as people will react to them in different ways. Clearly, the extent to which this is the case will vary between areas of research, projects and approaches, but it is difficult to avoid it totally, at least in qualitative studies. This means that methodological transparency must encompass an openness on the part of the researchers concerning their own sympathies and biases, as well as a clear statement of the approaches used. This has concomitant effects in terms of power relations and disciplinary scrutiny with which I am not entirely comfortable (Paechter 1996), but I think we may have to live with these for the sake of our research and its community.

Third, educational research, as with all research on human beings, should be conducted in ways that are explicitly ethically justifiable. Because much of our work is with children, this is something that we have to take particularly seriously. Again, this requires openness on the part of researchers and further scrutiny of our work, but again, it is necessary. Good ethical practice, however, is not just about how we treat our research participants, but how we treat each other. I particularly welcome moves towards reflective honesty in cases where researchers have found themselves to have been deceived, sometimes maliciously, by their informants (Sikes 2000); such honesty is difficult but ethically important.

I have not said anything here about the extent to which good educational research needs to be theoretically founded. This is because I am somewhat ambivalent about this. As a theorist myself, I value theory, and I think it is definitely beneficial for most educational research to have its roots in theoretical matters, and for researchers to be fully aware of, and open about, the theoretical underpinnings and implications of their findings. At the same time, I also believe that it is possible to build theory directly from empirical findings. So I think good educational research needs to have some relationship to theory, but that does not mean that it has to start from a theoretical position; it is reasonable for one to emerge from data as a result of a thoroughgoing analysis. However, we do need to rehabilitate theory among practitioners and, if possible, policy makers. Ball states:

> For me . . . theory provides the possibility of a different language, a language which is not caught up with the assumptions and inscriptions of policy-makers or the immediacy of practice (or embedded in tradition, prejudice, dogma and ideology . . .). It offers a potential location outside the prevailing discourses of policy and a way of struggling against 'incorporation'.
>
> (Ball 1997: 269)

It is not only educational researchers who need this alternative language; practitioners and their practices would benefit from it too.

I have said nothing so far about whether good educational research needs to resonate with or challenge, or otherwise relate to, those working in the (itself very broad) field of education. I have left this issue until this point because it is at the heart of this chapter. At first sight it seems to go without saying that, if those people directly involved in education (again interpreted broadly, to include teachers in a wide variety of educational institutions, including schools, further education colleges and universities, as well as policy makers, parents and learners) cannot relate to, agree with or see the point of a piece of research, then this is problematic. However, I want to argue later that this relationship between what one might call the producers of research, the research itself and the users of research, is complex and that expecting 'users' to be the judge of what matters may lead us away from forms of research that are in the long term very important. Furthermore, as Wilson and Wilson argue:

> Different concepts, or conceptions, or ideas, or 'paradigms' are associated with whatever we mark by the terms 'education' and 'research' themselves. Thus a person who has one conception of 'education' (and the same applies, to a lesser extent, to 'research') will present an idea of educational research which more or less *follows from* that conception;

> but this will not, as it were, 'speak to' or meet the mind of another person who has a different conception and hence sees educational research differently.
>
> (Wilson and Wilson 1998: 355)

Thus, in considering what makes a piece of educational research good, I am leaving aside the reactions to it of others involved in education; I will be arguing later that our understandings of utility make it a problematic criterion for judging the goodness or otherwise of a piece of educational or, indeed, other research.

Considering utility

It seems to me that an emphasis on utility is specific to certain areas of academic work and applies less to others. Education is, as I said earlier, one area in which usefulness is often regarded as being central to the purposes of research. I have also argued that this is at least in part due to the personal histories of the people who carry it out and the expectations of those working in the field being studied. Education is, after all, an applied discipline. However, there are contributory disciplines to the broad field of education, particularly philosophy and history, for which this requirement of utility is much less strong. Although it might be argued, for example, that we study history to learn lessons from the past, this would suggest that we might as a result choose to focus only on particular periods or themes; it is not immediately clear what relevance, for example, studying the technology of Roman Britain would have for the current practice of anything today. Rather, historians study history because it is interesting to them, and this is deemed acceptable by the general public because they also find history interesting (if only judging by the number of history-based television programmes screened each year).

This argument doesn't seem to be so acceptable for education, and not just because the general public doesn't seem to have the same intrinsic interest in the subject (although, of course, everyone has opinions about it). As an applied discipline, educational research is expected, by definition, to have some applicability to practice. How close that application needs to be, and what exactly we mean if we argue that educational research has to be useful, remains, however, a matter for debate.

In considering what we mean by 'useful' as it applies to educational research, there seem to be three broad categories that are used by researchers, policy makers and practitioners. These are:

- Immediate utility in schools – next week in my classroom (or someone else's).
- Immediate utility in terms of government policy – incorporated into policy soon.

- Furthering educational (or psychological or sociological or philosophical or historical) knowledge.

In considering these, we tend to prioritize the first two over the third, and the short over the long term. However, we need to ask whether this is necessarily a good thing (Hammersley 1997). This bias, of course, reflects the world in which educational researchers in many Western countries have been operating in the past twenty or so years. In England and Wales in particular, there have been rapid and successive changes in government policy, in terms both of curriculum and of pedagogy. Some of these have been more thoroughly based on research than others. What is certainly the case is that the frequency of change, some of it radical, has meant that, if research is to have any effect on either policy or practice, it has had to be very short-term. For example, much research carried out in England and Wales in the early 1990s (my own included) investigated a curriculum that was being changed by the government even as the research was being carried out (Paechter 2000b). Under such circumstances, in which the usefulness or otherwise of research is being judged in terms of very short-term needs and effects, it is difficult to argue that much educational research is useful at all: the processes of recognizing that something has to be investigated, obtaining funding, collecting and analysing data and then presenting conclusions simply takes longer than the policy cycle to which it is seen to apply. Prioritizing utility in such immediate terms is thus likely to militate against research that is good in the ways in which I outlined above. As Hammersley points out:

> One's attitude to the practical value of current educational research will depend a great deal on one's expectations about the contribution to practice that it *could* make. In my view . . . researchers have promised – and funders, policy-makers and practitioners have expected – too much; assuming that, in itself, research can provide practical solutions to practical problems.
>
> (Hammersley 1997: 149)

Expecting educational research to be of immediate practical relevance in a rapidly changing context is unrealistic. In these circumstances, the most useful contributions will be from those areas of the field often considered to be the most distant from practice: basic sociology, psychology and philosophy conducted in educational contexts. It is these areas, often considered to be the most 'ivory-tower', that can provide conclusions and ideas that remain applicable even as policy and practice undergo rapid changes.

These areas of educational research are, furthermore, those to which my third category of usefulness applies. It seems to me reasonable that at least part of the purpose of educational research is to contribute to the knowledge base of its contributing disciplines. In saying this I am not arguing, as do Wilson and Wilson (1998), that 'much goes on under the heading of "educational research" which is not, strictly speaking, about education at all' (p. 358). It is rather that, first, educational sites and situations are important social arenas whose investigation can contribute to our general knowledge about human beings and how they learn, behave and interact, and, second, this knowledge may, in the longer term, come back to be more directly relevant to the concerns of educational theorists and practitioners. To quote Hammersley again:

> The production of information of high practical relevance usually depends on a great deal of knowledge that does not have such relevance. In other words, for science to be able to contribute knowledge that is relevant to practice, a division of labour is required: a great deal of co-ordinated work is necessary tackling small, intermediate problems that do not have immediate pay-off. Moreover, this requires sustained work over a long period, not short bursts of activity geared to political and practical priorities.
>
> (Hammersley 1997: 146)

I do not think, however – nor, in my view, does Hammersley – that the division should be between those working in the foundational disciplines and those of us in departments of education or in schools. Researchers working in departments of education have a good deal to offer their originating disciplines, not least the cross-fertilization that comes from carrying out one's work alongside both practitioners and researchers in related disciplines. I shall say more about this below.

I want now to discuss a particular example of sociologically and psychologically based research, which while derided by practitioners as having little utility at the time it was published, has, in my view, proved its worth both in terms of its contribution to theory and in terms of its applicability to classroom practice. This particular example comes from a paradigm that I give the label 'deconstructive research'.

By 'deconstructive research' I mean research that seeks to question some of the assumptions behind discourses and practices – in this case, the discourses and practices of education. It looks at the ways we think about, for example, various classroom practices, and asks whether we could think about them differently and what the implications of this might be. A good example of deconstructive educational research is Valerie Walkerdine's (1984, 1988; Walkerdine and The Girls and Mathematics Unit 1989) work, in which she deconstructs the mathematical and other practices of primary and secondary classrooms. Walkerdine questions deeply held assumptions about what constitutes good mathematics, how power relations are enacted in classrooms and how the language of the primary classroom relates (or does not relate) to that of the home. To an educational researcher her work is fascinating, but to practitioners it has at times been extremely problematic. Mathematics educators, in particular, saw her writing, when it first appeared, as negative, critical of their teaching without offering any alternative approaches; the very opposite of useful.

I would argue, however, that in the longer term Walkerdine's work has had clear applications in practice, once the dust has settled and her ideas have been incorporated more into the 'thinking-as-usual' (Schutz 1964) of teacher educators and teachers. Ten to fifteen years on, her research is turning out to be extremely useful, both directly and indirectly. For example, her work on the use of tens and units blocks in teaching place value (Walkerdine 1988; Askew and William 1995) has clear implications for approaches to primary numeracy. Her demonstration of how and why mathematics teachers faced with tiered examination entry tend to enter male and female students for different levels has been taken on by other researchers, related to other work in assessment and used to show how this can prevent girls' having access to higher level examinations and, therefore, professional life chances (Walden and Walkerdine 1985; Walkerdine and The Girls and Mathematics Unit 1989; Gipps and Murphy 1994). Her work on the gendered nature of mathematics and how this applies to education has influenced researchers working both in gender and education and in mathematics education to such an extent that her ideas underpin much current work in both fields (e.g. Paechter 1998, 2000a; Francis 2000; Gates 2001; Skelton 2001). The problem, in these utility-focused times, is that we don't always know, when we carry out this sort of close and questioning scrutiny of educational situations and sites, if, or how, it will be useful – or how long it will take for this to happen. This is not, however, a sufficient reason for us to stop doing it.

How should we react to these tensions?

There is clearly a tension between the desire that a piece of educational research should be good and a requirement that it should also be immediately useful. This leads us to the question of how we, as educational researchers, should react to these opposing forces. It seems to me that we should rule out two possible answers immediately. The first of my rejected solutions is the suggestion that we should give more consideration to the practical concerns of particular audiences (Hillage *et al.* 1998). I do not think that it will be good either for educational research or, ultimately, for education practice if we increase our focus on the instantly useful. This is likely to lead to short-term projects, which, while they may address immediate problems, may only be able to do this at the expense of other important factors, such as ethical groundedness, rigour, clarity of approach and relation to theory.

My second rejected answer is one that, I have to admit, sometimes feels very tempting. Those educational researchers with strong ties to related disciplines such as sociology, psychology, philosophy or history, where researchers are far less frequently criticized for the lack of short-term applications for their work, could retreat into these areas, removing themselves from the field of education altogether. I don't think, however, that this is a good way forward, either for ourselves or for educational research. One of our strengths as educationalists is that our work often not only sits on the boundaries of these disciplines, but also crosses them. Walkerdine's work cited above, for example, straddles both deconstructive developmental psychology and sociology. Because of these marginal positions, we are often able to set the paradigms and understandings of a variety of disciplines and discourses against each other, with fruitful results both for theory and for practice. I think it would be a mistake if we were to lose this very important aspect of our work.

My (possibly radical) proposal is that, as educational researchers, we should focus on conducting good research in the field of education and trust to its utility. We are not always able to predict which areas will be most fertile for investigation, nor which studies will have most long-term impact. However, I think that anything that tells us more about the world of education (very broadly conceived) will be useful at some point. As long as we ensure that we carry out our work as well as it is possible to do so, with due regard to an underpinning moral imperative, rigour, transparency, connection to theory and research ethics, we will be contributing to knowledge in the field of education. This should be our purpose.

Notes

1 This is not to imply that teachers should not carry out educational research. It is the case, however, that most do not.

2 The distinction between empirical and scholarly work is clearly not in practice as sharp as I am drawing it here. Empirical research can, for example (as does Walkerdine's work discussed below), result in analyses that relate more closely to the 'scholarly' outcomes I describe than to the directly useful results expected and desired by practitioners and policy makers.

3 This is an exercise undertaken every five years in the UK in which university departments submit accounts of their research work, together with lists of publications, to specialist panels, who are then expected to judge the standing of the department as a whole in terms of its research. It is currently a central aspect of university life in the UK, both as a measure of departmental standing and as a major conduit for funding.

References

Askew, M. and William, D. (1995) *Recent Research in Mathematics Education 5–16*. London: HMSO.

Ball, S.J. (1997) Policy sociology and critical social research: a personal view of recent educational policy and policy research, *British Educational Research Journal*, 23(3): 257–74.

Francis, B. (2000) *Boys, Girls and Achievement: Addressing the Classroom Issues*. London: Routledge Falmer.

Gates, P. (ed.) (2001) *Issues in Mathematics Teaching*. London: Routledge Falmer.

Gipps, C. and Murphy, P. (1994) *A Fair Test? Assessment, Achievement and Equity*. Buckingham: Open University Press.

Hammersley, M. (1997) Educational research and teaching: a response to David Hargreaves' TTA lecture, *British Educational Research Journal*, 23(2): 141–61.

Hargreaves, D. (1996) Teaching as a research-based profession: possibilities and prospects. *Teacher Training Agency Annual Lecture*, London, March.

Higher Education Funding Council for England (2001) *2001 Research Assessment Exercise: The Outcomes*. London: HEFC.

Hillage, J., Pearson, R., Anderson, A. and Tamkin, P. (1998) *Excellence in Research on Schools: Research Summary*. London: Department for Education and Employment.

Mortimore, P. (2000) Does educational research matter?, *British Educational Research Journal*, 26(1): 5–24.

Paechter, C.F. (1996) Power, knowledge and the confessional in qualitative research, *Discourse: Studies in the Cultural Politics of Education*, 17(1): 75–84.

Paechter, C.F. (1998) *Educating the Other: Gender, Power and Schooling*. London: Falmer Press.

Paechter, C.F. (2000a) *Changing School Subjects: Power, Gender and Curriculum*. Buckingham: Open University Press.

Paechter, C.F. (2000b) Moving with the goalposts: carrying out curriculum research in a period of constant change, *British Educational Research Journal*, 26(1): 27–39.

Schutz, A. (1964) The stranger, in B.R. Cosin, I.R. Dale, G.M. Esland, D. MacKinnon and D.F. Swift (eds) *School and Society*. London: Routledge & Kegan Paul.

Sikes, P. (2000) 'Truth' and 'lies' revisited, *British Educational Research Journal*, 26(2): 257–70.

Skelton, C. (2001) *Schooling the Boys: Masculinities and Primary Education*. Buckingham: Open University Press.

Tooley, J. and Darby, D. (1998) *Educational Research – A Critique*. London: Office for Standards in Education.

Walden, R. and Walkerdine, V. (1985) *Girls and Mathematics: From Primary to Secondary Schooling*. London: Heinemann.

Walkerdine, V. (1984) Developmental psychology and the child-centred pedagogy: the insertion of Piaget into early education, in J. Henriques, W. Hollway, C. Urwin, C. Venn and V. Walkerdine (eds) *Changing the Subject*. London: Methuen.

Walkerdine, V. (1988) *The Mastery of Reason*. Cambridge: Routledge & Kegan Paul.

Walkerdine, V. and The Girls and Mathematics Unit (1989) *Counting Girls Out*. London: Virago.

Wilson, J. and Wilson, N. (1998) The subject-matter of educational research, *British Educational Research Journal*, 24(3): 355–63.

8 | Method and morality: practical politics and the science of human affairs

Fred Inglis

> To ask questions you see no prospect of answering is the fundamental sin in science, like giving orders which you do not think will be obeyed in politics, or praying for what you do not think God will give in religion.
>
> (R.G. Collingwood)

A particular historical and political circumstance calls for a response from all those who continue to suppose that education is a moral process in which free, present or future citizens acquire the accomplishments necessary to make a living for themselves and other people, while at the same time learning to handle, judge and criticize the experiences they live through by way of a set of more or less intellectual instruments and frameworks provided by that education. Such frameworks may be thought of as offering intelligible form to the contents of history; such a formulation not only comprises a hermeneutic for the passions, it also requires the identification of values (conceived here as little local intensities of *meaning*) as the inevitable context of factual description.

Putting things like this not only presumes the final dissolution of any absolute boundary between body, mind and emotion in methodological argument (since each is alike the ground of being), it also commits us to the endorsement of John Searle's argument[1] that language of its nature configures significance; that is to say, concepts, in giving form to phenomena, energize the (factual) phenomena with a human charge.

Accordingly, to discuss education is simply to rejoin the conversation of the human sciences as that conversation was animatedly resumed at the dead end of the positivist detour sometime in the 1950s, when positivism itself, whether logical or physicalist became, as far as human inquiry was conceived, disintegrated under the attacks of Quine and Davidson. At that same moment, and not coincidentally, a new wave of humanist criticism swept in on the same tide. It was inspired, in the case of one leading figure in the movement, Jurgen Habermas, by the determination to reclaim the Hegelian–Heideggerian tradition of public moralizing from the contaminations of Fascism, and in two of its Anglophone examples, Charles Taylor and Alisdair MacIntyre, a similar impulse was at work to restore to Marx the best of his non-deterministic radicalism.

There was, as it happened, a home-grown voice contemporary with the advocates of a hard realism in moral philosophy and historical inquiry. All through the inter-war years, R.G. Collingwood had, in a prodigious series of books,[2] some only published in fragments after his death, pressed home the necessity of his 'question-and-answer-logic' upon a heedless audience. History was, in his book, queen of the sciences, in the sense that prior experience formed us all and all our social institutions, and that therefore the only way to understand the mess things are in is to discover how they got to be that way in the first place.

Hence question-and-answer logic. Collingwood's historical method was to seek to recover the original questions implicit in the answers found in any piece of evidence: a book of political theory, a painting, broken shards found at an archaeological dig, each alike constituted an embodied answer, not necessarily satisfactory, to questions put to experience by the matter. Such a move placed human purposes and intentions, their reasons and motives, at the heart of the science of affairs. The deep puzzle for human beings is to make sense of experience, to turn a meaningless sequence of accidents tumbling out of the future into an action that may be controlled and an event that may be understood.

In his endeavours, Collingwood may be said to be doing no more than systematize the procedures of everyday life. There can hardly be, nonetheless, a happier or more rational justification for a human science. Collingwood had formed his ambition to connect intelligent theory to deranged practices during his duties at the Admiralty between 1914 and 1918, when the lack of any such connection was so decidedly noticeable. But no sooner was that most avoidable, irrational and mortally extravagant of human undertakings over, than philosophers set off again on their madly irrelevant dance to turn humanity into the objects of a natural science which could only be successful in regulating conduct by removing alike both reason and passion.

It seemed to Collingwood and, gradually, to his successors in the business of theorizing human fatheadedness, that the best way forward would be to sort into order the commonplace procedures whereby we all try to explain what people (including ourselves) are up to. We regard their actions and listen to their utterances, searching in the contexts of their conduct for the meaning in their minds. By these familiar tokens, individual biography is always relevant but never enough. Settling text into context without allowing explanation to dissolve into circumstantiality is the concern of the circling hermeneutician and whatever may be said by the frivolous jesters of postmodernism[3] about the sheer impossibility of recovering other people's intentions, there simply is no other available practice of mind with which to make sense of the world.

No doubt to put things *quite* so plainly and bluntly is a self-deception. There is no set distance at which the hermeneutician is best placed to begin his or her circling. Too near to the human action in question and you are held too tightly in the forcefield of a few individuals; too far and you lose the exhilarating wrestle with human quiddity. Soporific old bromides about the woods and the trees have their pedagogic force, and every inquiry has to settle for its partial and partisan vision.

Thus the historian reconstructs from the primary sources the day-to-day exigencies whereby, let us say, the extremely poor proletariat of nineteenth-century industrialization made out or went under. Such a book is Eric Hobsbawm's and George Rudé's *Captain Swing*[4] or, more immediately, Friedrich Engels' great classic of 1844, *The Condition of the Working Class in England*. Another historian, as close as he can get to the immediacies of the daily record of immiseration and revolt, then draws back to the boundary set by a different interpretative rim – one moreover only made accessible by an unplannable coincidence of luck, moral allegiance, good wits and the right, but unpredictable historical distance from the original. At this distance, with these gifts, E.P. Thompson described[5] not only the daily life of weavers and wool-pickers and loom-makers, he saw in it the coming-to-consciousness-of-itself of a new presence on the stage of history, the English working class. By the time he wrote his great book, that class had come to its maturity as a long-standing political force in the march of the nation, and was in a position to grasp and interpret the significance of its beginnings.

Let us take another example closer to our educational headquarters. In 1962, two sociologists, both with working-class origins and political allegiances, published a study of what it meant for bright children from similar backgrounds to have won places, by virtue of the mildly egalitarian Education Act of 1944, at their local grammar school. These, of course, had been formerly the pretty well exclusive preserve of the respectable middle classes in the neighbourhood – the solicitors, accountants, businessmen, dentists and, indeed, schoolteachers – who regarded the school as their imperium.

Brian Jackson and Dennis Marsden[6] set themselves, according to conventions of social inquiry of the time, to interview (without tape recorder) a number of former grammar school boys and girls, mainly from working-class homes, although a few had middle-class backgrounds, as well as a selection of their parents.

This may be thought of as inquiry of the first order or of biographical immediacy. What the two authors recounted was a vivid, sometimes comic tale of the 'symbolic violence' (the phrase belongs to Pierre Bourdieu) wrought by social class ritual and middle-class presumption upon the interlopers who had broken open the class boundary. For the first time outside the English novel (a key resource for social theorists), what Raymond Williams famously conceptualized as 'structures of feeling' came into rancorous and unresolved class conflict in the pages of social inquiry. The struggle was fought out over social emancipation, and morally, of course, the working class wins. But the point of all this for the methodist of inquiry was that the two men couldn't tell a tale without a narrative tension between how the world was and how it ought to have been.

This is not the case, as hardly needs saying, in natural-scientific modes of conjecture and refutation (in Popper's canonical phrase). According to protocol, the laboratory scientist approaches phenomena with a hypothesis and proceeds until the hypothesis is falsified. Thomas Kuhn has taught us that this is far from being the real life of scientists, many of whom hang onto their paradigm in the teeth of unaccommodatable evidence for as long as it takes. Clive James immortally characterized this more familiar kind of obstinacy as being the history of science as taught by television dramatizations, whereby a lot of whitebearded old men are proved (gradually) wrong by one man with a black beard.

The television scientists remind us of real life. Popper's classical sequence describes the ideal type of scientific investigation. It is, however, the relevance of my historical and sociological examples that hypothesis-testing in human affairs is simply impossible. For years it was insisted upon as protocol for unhappy doctoral students, and for years the dissertations rolled in with the conclusion that the hypothesis was partly true and partly wasn't. When the slow shift of the human scientific paradigm began to take place, the contention emerged that the explanation of conduct, however near or far the explicator might be from the subject and object-matter, could only make sense if conduct were to be measured against the goals, the purposes and interactions of the agent.

Such an approach would deploy question-and-answer logic with a teleological vengeance. For while motive or intention (the two not synonymous, motive being antecedent to action and intention embodied in it[7]) may pertain to quite modest activities as well as grand ambitions, a goal is a distinctly more resonant object of aspiration. The answer to questions of experience provided by the attainment of a goal is likely to be a roundly existential affair. One scores one's big life-goals, if one is lucky, in the name of the big commitments to value.

There can only be dispute about the identity of these values. Isaiah Berlin has shown us that, by way of historical and anthropological revelation, specific human values are incompatible just as their very meaning and structure (Gallie's famous claim[8]) may be inherently contestable. Nonetheless, although the lesson is now well learned that values are always disputable, my commonplace argument here will be that all research in the human sciences, but supremely in educational matters, can only provide explanations by adducing as a comparative framework, a state of affairs in some way morally alternative (or transcendental) to the one under investigation.

Thus the psychologist studies cognitive styles against a criterion of efficient thinking; a historian reviews battles and parliaments in terms of victory or defeat, successfully or fallibly handled power; an anthropologist has in mind, however relatively, a picture of what it is for social ceremony to function well (functionalism), for social structure to match form to ontology fittingly (structuralism), for social intercourse and spectacular display to be carried off convincingly (symbolic action theory); an educationist, whether managerialist, stern inspector or old utopian, tests the school for the way it lives a picture of the good society, courteous, assiduous, equitable, variegated, orderly.

II

The comparative dualism of social-theoretic analysis and its unavoidable evaluations has still, however, an impossible time affirming its sheer necessity against the mammoth continuity of a view of social – or, as I prefer, human – science resting on the old delusions of scientific positivism and physicalism. It should by now be plain as day that the mindless antinomies between quantitative and qualitative research, subjective and objective data and findings, between facts and values themselves, are long since dissolved and superseded.

The continued fixity of the fact-value distinction owes much to Max Weber's methodological insistence on their separation.[9] The qualitative–quantitative opposition is partly a consequence of the divisions of labour and the protection of academic mystery (statistics are difficult to a still innumerate society, even in the academies) and partly grounded in the old faith in science and Comtean scientism – the belief that scientific method having brought so much simple benefit by way of surgery, pharmacology, engineering, technological communication and modern weaponry, it ought to be entrusted with doing the same for human organization. As for the preference for so-called objective observation-and-experiment over subjective participation-and-anguish, that seems to me simply a failure of intelligence, though also one caused by too great a faith in the knife, the microscope and the book of sums. Nothing by this date, surely, is more fatuous than a failure to grasp the irreducible nature of intersubjective interaction. To study people in society is to study them in exchange with one another, never more so than in the unbelievable but comprehensible babel of electronic communication, the silent accurate clamour of which announces the advent of Manuel Castells' 'information age'.[10] To bring to bear the laborious separations of subjective and objective on the global *suq* is to condemn oneself to bewilderment as surely as if one were a bushman.

But people *will* still do it, and it is a pedagogic necessity of a book such as this one that it rehearse the history and contrivance of the intellectual position it defends. After all, vast research awards are still made in the rich countries of the world on the basis of these ancient intellectual instruments. For it is the general case that, in the human sciences at large, the representation of the real world that wins the money without even having to argue against the others is what is believed to be the standardly scientific version: that matching of facts-turned-into-figures against an unproblematic reality which is positivism. By its lights, carefully selected figures (data) translated from linguistically specified attitudes (selected on a five-point scale) may be used to test for the presence or absence of hypothetic values or competences in the society (falsifiability). Thus citizens are judged to have reported on key issues in the polity by the same methods that small children are found to be linguistically incompetent as a consequence of not talking to them carefully enough. What is risible about this state of affairs is that identical methods are applied to entirely unalike circumstances precisely in the name of being scientific.

The privilege of such representations is, as is usual with privilege, first evident in wealth. Research funds flow to those who do research according to the paradigms of normal social science. Since power of its nature exacts deference and imitation, privileged representation expects to have its rhetorical demands met. Moreover, and as a residue from Marxism, even those who repudiate scientism nonetheless style themselves sanctimonious materialists, because its purported opposite of idealism is supposed to characterize liberal-bourgeois social theory and its innate deference to the *status quo*.

To note these status skirmishes is not to launch an attack upon the idea of science. Science will make its advances in its incremental way, and its canons of evidence, disengagement, authority and the rest, for all their sociability, will continue to win their objective successes. What has been dislodged by the philosophic warrening of the past thirty years has been the privileged representation of reality by the mirror epistemological theory. Whatever the serenity of day-to-day scientific practice, the inclusive idea that language can faithfully and truly mirror the phenomena of the factual world-out-there has splintered under the impact of sceptical and deconstructive arguments.

The mirror metaphor is Richard Rorty's and he is field-marshal of the philosophic efforts that have broken it up. The mirror is suggested by the first premise of classical epistemology, which Rorty summarizes thus: 'Whenever we make an incorrigible report on a state of ourselves [or of Nature], there must be a property with which we are presented which induces us to make this report'.[11] This premise is common to normal science as well as to the self-styled cultural materialists of cultural studies. Rorty, however, is genially dismissive of the idea that the world is divided up into only two ways of seeing it, idealism and materialism. For him and for me theoretic understanding is a matter of discovering (and in part *inventing*) a sufficiently truthful narrative with which to frame the facts:

> There are two principal ways in which reflective human beings try, by placing their lives in a larger context, to give sense to those lives. The first is by telling the story of their contribution to a community. This community may be the actual historical one in which they live, or another actual one, distant in time or place, or a quite imaginary one, consisting perhaps of a dozen heroes and heroines selected from history or fiction or both. The second way is to describe themselves as standing in an immediate relation to a non-human reality. This relation is immediate in the sense that it does not derive from a relation between such a reality and their tribe, or their nation, or their imagined band of comrades. I shall say that stories of the former kind exemplify the desire for solidarity, and that stories of the latter kind exemplify the desire for objectivity.[12]

Surprisingly, it is then possible to summon up help from the hardest of the unregenerate physicalists.

In his 'Two dogmas of empiricism',[13] William Quine attacks the foundation dogmas of normal social science and leaves it bereft of its central quantity, what Rorty calls its 'glassy essence' ('glassy essence' being the reflection of reality caught in the mental mirror polished with its language by the mind).

Quine first dissolves Kant's classical distinction between analytic propositions (those which we know 'incorrigibly' as matters of observed or introspective fact) and synthetic propositions (where statements are true 'tautologically' as a result of the definition of their terms: a triangle is a three-sided figure). Secondly, he challenges the empirical dogma that every statement is a construction from immediate experience.

He contends that all inquiry is intrinsically holistic; it works within a *set* of propositions not down an agenda. Each proposition is no more than an element in a system, and as such is always correctable, and may indeed have to be abandoned completely (as constantly happens not just to explanations but to facts in science). So much for analytic truth. But, relatedly, synthetic truths cannot be *proved* tautologically, because no definition or synonym can be shown to be a perfect translation of the first term. Translation or synonymity is too slippery a criterion with which to fix perfect synthetic propositions. Thus the second dogma perishes.[14]

This is to represent much-disputed conclusions in rather a sharp-shooting way. Rorty uses Quine to reject flat-footed materialists who want to say that all human activity may be explained without remainder as the product of neural processes, as well as the so-called dualists for whom the body is one physical thing and the mind another, immaterial or 'ghostly' thing. As I remarked, Rorty asks sarcastically, 'What is this mental–physical contrast anyway? Whoever said that anything one mentioned had to fall into one or other of two (or half-a-dozen) ontological realms?'[15]

If this sounds too breezy, let us concede the triumph of material explanation but ask what it looks like. Is it a matter of having correctly described mental actions? If so, that's not much of a victory. For one may be easily able to predict individual actions or even one day to pick up by way of some science-fictional radio attached to the cortex whatever thoughts are passing through someone's mind, without the police being any the wiser. Even at that pitch of surveillance, thoughts, words and concepts will require interpretation and all interpretation is challengeable.

There is just no *need* to keep the fight going between the two titans of the nineteenth-century human sciences, materialism and idealism. Rorty offers to finish off the distinction with Quine's help and that of Wilfred Sellars. Human knowledge does not have to be, in Rorty's phrase, an 'assemblage of representations in a mirror of nature'[16] and if we can so dispense with the mirror, we can dispense with the mind–body problem and 'the mystery concerning the relation of that mirror to our grosser parts'.

Rorty, it should be said, is the most forceful representative of that radical tendency in thought to call doubt on all our systems of representation in thought. However, it would be quite wrong to classify a man of his ilk as deconstructionist, where that term designates the calculated subversion of intentional meaning by the discovery of unintendedly contrary or subversive meanings. Instead, Rorty enlists Wilfred Sellars to profess a view of knowledge and truth as (in Dewey's phrase) 'warranted assertability', and the business of justification of either truth or knowledge is not a special and privileged court of appeal at which all the rest of the conversation is cross-examined and sentenced.

Sellars aims to finish with 'the myth of the given'.[17] If we want to know something about a person's internal states – for example, whether they are in pain – only a philosopher would be suspicious about asking the person and believing the answer. But the authority of philosophy is such that we worry about the status of such replies as soon as we start doing a human science. There need be nothing 'lying behind' any such reply because the convention of trustworthy replying is constituted by the common meaningfulness and conversational understanding of being in pain. Such reports – 'ow, that hurts' – are, in the jargon, 'incorrigible' because there is (so far) no better method of determining what is the case than to believe what someone says.

All this may seem very heavy weather to make of what everybody knows

– what is, in the excellent phrase, common knowledge. But that is Rorty's great point, and the means whereby he wants *all* the sciences to swing from an epistemological perch to a hermeneutic one. Sellars recommends that we free ourselves from always sternly insisting that our consciousness (whatever *that* is), our sense-impressions, our cognitions and concepts (whatever *they* are) have to find some foundation outside language and society before we can say anything definite about them. By implication, therefore, Sellars endorses not historicism – the belief that history is on the march to somewhere – but historicality as our real foundation. Our consciousness and our concepts are folded upon us by the slow accumulations of time. We can trace this process of the formation of mind and its modes of perception historically, and when we have done so, in Sellars's view, there is no remainder called the grounding-of-knowledge-in-reality still to be accounted for.

This doesn't mean that there is no such thing as progress; and it certainly doesn't mean that the vulgar relativist can pop up again and say that for people who believe in witchcraft, there are truly witches, and that *The Exorcist* may indeed tell a true story. It is to show that all you need to disprove black magic are the everyday conventions of observation, proof and scepticism. As I also suggested in the wake of Sellars, charges of idealism turn out either to be vacuous or mere platitudes. If idealism is supposed to mean that the bourgeoisie recreates the world of entities by giving them the names which suit it, then it is vacuous. If, on the other hand, it is supposed to mean the way in which we do our best to join our language intelligibly to our world, and to ensure a rational-sounding continuity between past and present beliefs about and methods of inquiry, then we shall all have to get used to being idealists.

In Quine's famous formulation for sceptics, all theories are underdetermined by the facts, and the best that we can do to fix both is to talk about our whole way of talking about the world. This leaves us in a paradox, that while having treated with grave doubts the efforts made in the human and natural sciences accurately to represent in language the world-out-there, we nonetheless intend in future to treat the realm of that whole conversation, with all its games of language and constituent forms of life, as our oyster. If this conversation is not subject and object of our study (which would be impossible), then it is the unignorable context of the pearly topics that are embedded in it.

The study of education, conceived at its grandest, is therefore the study of the conversation of humankind (Oakeshott's great phrase), but in particular that part of the conversation that creates and ratifies the form and content of official knowledge, the protocols of inquiry, and the formal values of the society which permits the conversation in the first place.

III

On such a definition, the field of research and the subject-matter of education are set embarrassingly wider than is presently countenanced by the wizened agoraphobics who allocate research grants and dissertation topics. To treat education so largely (however sectionally as you go along) is to take in the self-broadcasting of a society.

To use the term is to force home the polemic. The key contribution of the mighty historical and cultural researches associated with the names of Richard Hoggart and Raymond Williams, Edward Thompson and Eric Hobsbawm, is that they insist upon the world-shaping and world-shaking powers of *both* educated and customary knowledge. In the present, it is banal to observe, both categories are everywhere present in the broadcast knowledges of the classroom, as they are in the broadcast knowledges of what we more usually know as broadcast*ing*. The study of the practices of education, if it is to be any more than managing the machinery of schooling, is the study of the meanings and values embodied in the overlapping conversation of educational institutions and educative television (very broadly defined).

Like a literature, a legislature, a military or a social class, an education is made visible in the mighty frescoes of culture as, in Clifford Geertz's phrase, 'a constellation of enshrined ideas'.[18] Even more far-reachingly, for it purports to reflect a nation talking to itself and speaking peace to other nations, the conversation of television enshrines a society's best imaginary efforts to bring out the best in itself. The assiduous researcher, who must be, at the same time, a social and intellectual critic of that society, is working to map that constellation, discover its shrines and criticize its ideas. He or she can only do so by projecting a not-very-distant future in which the best ideas and values as imagined on behalf of the present may have some chance of coming-to-fulfilment in the lives of the successor generation.

Such research – let us say, such humanly necessary self-aware self-criticism – is historicist in so far as it understands present circumstances as a product of past stupidity or intelligence, and futurist, according to historical Enlightenment principles, in so far as it attaches policy to politics by way of trying for a just and trustworthy emancipation of its optimistic youth.

Obviously, such a programme needs more sophisticated instruments of analysis than I have so far adumbrated here. Educational knowledge systems, and the evaluative structure they entail and express through such innumerable manifestations as their hierarchies and rewards, their appraisive procedures and their practical symbolism and manners, speak eloquently of a society's answers to the question, 'how shall we live? *what for* – what ultimately do we live for?' If we turn for help to Basil Bernstein's distinction between vertical and horizontal discourses,[19] we begin to make the vitalizing connection between the rigours of a science of human affairs and the delight and anguish of living out the human experience itself.

The abominable failing of social science in its positivist mode was to kill the life it studied; the corresponding sentimentality of those who exalted a so-called phenomenology of experience was to suppose that such representation permitted understanding. Bernstein provides a new classification of knowledge and its values, in which the horizontal structure is marked off in the segments of everyday life, its specializations and competences all as defined by context and necessity. In vertical discourses, however, knowledge-and-value is assigned in a sequence of graded performances individually acquired under official surveillance, and in which the implicit principle of distribution becomes articulate as a discipline of recontextualization. Segments exclude in the name of practice; hierarchies include under the badge of theory. In every case, what Bernstein calls 'the pedagogic device' grasps the new thought-never-before-thought and 'recontextualizes' it.

It is obvious that the knowledge system of television broadcasting is as amenable to such analysis as those of schools or universities. Television cookery classes are horizontal and segmental, television history hierarchical and theoretic. *Both*, however, may transpire in new thought and more often on television than in a classroom or seminar room, where the *point* of the knowledge communicated is to conserve itself, and to sustain the reproduction of the society in the future.

Either way, however, the necessary, life-enhancing study of these zones of human conduct can only take place under the irreducible sign of human intersubjectivity. That is the main text of this essay and it is, in origin, Wittgenstein's. Wittgenstein put away the sentimentalists of sacredly personal experience in a simple homily:

> The temptation to say 'I see it like *this*', pointing to the same thing for 'it' and 'this'. Always get rid of the idea of a private object in this way: assume that it constantly changes, but that you do not notice the change because your memory constantly deceives you.[20]

So much for the subjectivists. But Wittgenstein goes on,[21]

> If language is to be a means of communication, there must be agreement not only in definitions but also (queer as this sounds) in judgements. This seems to abolish logic, but does not do so.

Wittgenstein's contention is that only in the shared and public usages of language and its historically constituted meanings can we find out what people are up to; my corollary is that, once they are interpreted, we can only then criticize their actions in terms of the best those agents could have thought and said for themselves.

Wittgenstein has, however, one further admonition to make to us about our understanding of others' actions. It is one which not only – to my mind

– disables almost all academic psychology, but also and more widely provides a touchstone for the methodological argument commended here:

> try not to think of understanding as a 'mental process' at all – for that is the expression which confused you. But ask yourself: in what sort of case, in what kind of circumstances do we say, 'Now I know how to go on', when that is, the formula *has* occurred to me? In the sense in which there are processes (including mental processes) which are characteristic of understanding, understanding is not a mental process.[22]

We know how to go on with a calculation when we recall the formula we need. We know what people are doing when an interpretative framework fits the action. In addition, we sometimes may calculate, or we may interpret in a hitherto unthinkable way; when we do so, we fetch out, through our *inventive* powers, the combinations of convention and novelty, potentiality and custom, concentration and expansion, which have been hitherto unperceived and which, once made visible, provide the grounds for human and social betterment in the future.

IV

So far, so good. But the psychologism in the middle of Romantic thought put a sacred value on inner states and the immanence of personal feeling, and fixed the fight as forever between hard-faced objectivists and soft-nosed subjectivists. This cut off the public nature of language from the private space of desire. The Romantics won the day for art, music and poetry as the domain of personal redemption; in doing so, they insisted (in the theodicy which was their inheritance) that grace was ineffable and works alone could not save.

The consequences of this for the phenomenology of educational research were that any pupil might be saved by the pentecost of true personal feeling but that you couldn't truly tell from what they wrote or said. The belief augmented an admirable respect for all pupils as possessed of moral feeling, but it made a mistake about language. If we correct the mistake by borrowing from a different way of thinking, we can launch a usable and useful model of inquiry that may stop the present destructiveness of contention and still keep faith with the best allegiances of emancipatory research. This is how the reinvention of tradition (and theory) works; this is our vocation.

The way of thinking in question is here attributed to Wittgenstein. Understanding is, so to speak, a cooperative concept. This sorts with Wittgenstein's difficulty about understanding. We say, 'I understand how you feel' when the process of understanding is hidden from us.

But we *do* understand how they feel. That is because we understand what they say, *not* by way of a 'mental process', for as we have seen, psychological words do not name 'private experiences which we alone can know'. We do our understanding by way of the language, which, like other signs and symbols not our business, inveigles meaning and is organized for our purposes into texts.

The conduct of educational research is therefore the study of its 'language-games', in Wittgenstein's famous phrase. We start with the enormous field upon which the games are played and study them to determine what the rules are, and – in another powerful phrase of his – what 'forms of life' they shape and inform.

The main help I aim to win from this formula is that, in ordering research inquiry, we do not have to invoke or speculate about 'inner states', any more than we must profess an inhuman objectivity. The public arrangement of language into texts is all our concern, and if this peculiar attentiveness puts the psychoanalytical school of textual study out of business, then about time, too.

Such a formula, in spite of the best efforts of the dottier exponents of postmodernism, cannot ignore or discount what people purposed or intended in what they said or wrote. It has been the second great discovery about language made by philosophers and students of literature alike that words are *not*, as it were, lenses that may be ground so finely we can see the world through them with such clarity that what we see is what is really there. Language is a set of instruments with which to do things and when, writing at the same time as Wittgenstein, John Austin wrote *How to Do Things with Words*, the force of that 'do' was what he wanted to bring out.

Alongside the rules of the games, therefore, is the point of the games, or an answer to the question, 'What are people doing when they say that?' Austin coined the neologism 'performatives'[23] to cover this aspect of language, or, rather, these forces in the linguistic field. Thus, when I say 'I promise' or 'I surrender', I am not making a true or false proposition about the world, I am *doing* something. The three forces of language Austin distinguished were: its locutionary force (lexical meaning, or what the words *tell*); its illocutionary force (performative meaning, or what the words *do*); and its perlocutionary force (persuasive meaning, or what the words *effect*).

We begin, I hope, to see the outlines of that model of language which also provides us with a methodological sequence. We learn the rules and with them we also learn how to play the game well: how to do things.

But these actions have a history. People have not always done things with words that way. The rules themselves have changed from time to time. The history of our language is the history of our human constitution, but that is not to say that we are each constituted by the sheer weight of linguistic sedimentation. Sentences conserve meaning; they also radicalize meaning. We use words and concepts (the two terms far from being the same thing) in such a way as to separate an old from a new meaning ('literature', for example, may happily mean either an advertising brochure or a great novel). Inquiry into the worlds people make in virtue of the words that they speak must include glimpses of their common history.

Structure; performance; history; *values*. This last is the fourth realm of my model of inquiry; it gathers up all the others. It wouldn't be difficult to connect some such model up to levels of achievement and key stages if you have to do such a thing, as long as we keep clearly in mind Jerome Bruner's strictures on Piaget. Bruner reminds us that stages of development have no epistemological foundation and that intellectual (and, come to that, emotional) development is always recursive, provisional, moody, contextual. (Are you as bright as you were last year?)

By values I indicate those concentrations of meaning whereby language makes its 'distinctions of worth' (Charles Taylor's phrase). We live on ground marked out by such distinctions; we are constituted by them; and given that they are made in language, then by our prior arguments, these distinctions cannot be private or merely subjective, still less may they be abstract realities. Our values live in the language of the day. They are texts to be read, and read intersubjectively; disputed intersubjectively also no doubt, but disputed in terms of common human meanings. Valuing, then, is not a mental or emotional process, it is a symbolic action and, as Clifford Geertz says:

> The confinement of interpretive analysis . . . to the supposedly more 'symbolic' aspect of culture is a mere prejudice, born out of the notion, also a gift of the 19th century, that 'symbolic' opposes to 'real' as fanciful to sober, figurative to liberal, obscure to plain, aesthetic to practical, mystical to mundane, and decorative to substantial.[24]

We trace our values, which are no more and no less than the meanings of life, through our linguistic – that is, our symbolic – texts. The best way of gathering the whole enormous venture under one heading is to say that we study that 'ensemble of stories we tell ourselves about ourselves',[25] which simply *is* culture, and study it with a view to our deciding which stories are good for us and which bad, and what the new stories we create for ourselves may do for either end.

Intellectual method cannot promise genius, but it should at least forestall stupidity. In so far as it is successful, it should also be beautiful, which for our purposes means that educational inquiry be a branch of literature. If we read John Dewey or even Pierre Bourdieu at his most serenely difficult, they match such a standard. The sheer laughability of applying it to the usual run of the subject brings out the occasion for this essay. Our common pursuit is no less than to find, and in finding to invent, a sufficiently truthful *recit de nos jours*. The *grands recits* are, as we know, over. We are in a period similar to other such historical periods (the Reformation, for instance) which measures a marked acceleration in the desuetude of narratives. The grand task, one quite enough to make one's heart swell and blood run quick, is to help contrive out of the facts of the matter an everyday story about education that will help students and teachers alike to do right and live well.

Notes

1 In John Searle (1995) *The Construction of Social Reality*. London: Allen Lane; this is a careful inversion of the famous predecessor title by John Berger and Thomas Luckmann (1971) *The Social Construction of Reality*. Harmondsworth: Penguin.

2 The most succinct of which is, for our purposes, the *Autobiography* (Oxford: Clarendon Press, 1938). See also, of course, *The Principles of Art* (1938), *The Idea of History* (1946) and the *Essay on Metaphysics* (1940), all published by Clarendon Press.

3 In particular, Jacques Derrida (1979) *Spurs: Nietzsche's Styles*. Chicago, IL: University of Chicago Press, pp. 123, 125, 127, 131.

4 Hobsbawm, E. and Rude, G. (1969) *Captain Swing*. London: Lawrence & Wishart.

5 Thompson, E.P. (1968) *The Making of the English Working Class*. Harmondsworth: Penguin (revised edition).

6 Jackson, B. and Marsden, D. (1966) *Education and the Working Class*. Harmondsworth: Penguin (revised edition).

7 A distinction I follow from Quentin Skinner (1989) Motives, intentions and the interpretations of texts, reprinted in *Meaning and Context* (J. Tully, ed.). Cambridge: Polity Press.

8 Gallie, W.B. (1968) *Philosophy and Historical Understanding*. New York: Schocken Books.

9 Weber, M. (1949) *The Methodology of the Social Sciences*. New York: Free Press (first published 1903–1917).

10 Castells, M. (1998) *The Information Age: Economy, Society and Culture*, Vol. III, *End of Millennium*. Oxford: Blackwell.

11 Rorty, R. (1981) *Philosophy and the Mirror of Nature*. Oxford: Blackwell, p. 100.

12 Rorty, R. (1985) Solidarity or objectivity?, in J. Rajchman and C. West (eds) *Post-analytic Philosophy*. New York: Columbia University Press, pp. 3–19.

13 Quine, W.V.O. (1980) Two dogmas of empiricism, in *From a Logical Point of View*. Cambridge, MA: Harvard University Press (revised edition), pp. 37–46.

14 The synonymity paradox is developed in Quine, W.V.O. (1960) On the indeterminacy of translation, in *Word and Object*. Boston, MA: MIT Press. See also Dunn, J. (1978) Practising social science on realist assumptions, in *Political Obligation in its Historical Context*. Cambridge: Cambridge University Press.

15 Rorty, op. cit., note 11, pp. 122–3.

16 Rorty, op. cit., note 11, pp. 126–7.

17 Sellars, W. (1963) *Silence, Perception and Reality*. Cambridge, MA: Harvard University Press.
18 Geertz, C. (1981) *Negara: The Theatre-state in 19 Century Bali*. Princeton, NJ: Princeton University Press, p. 135.
19 Bernstein, B. (2000) *Pedagogy, Symbolic Control and Identity: Theory, Research, Critique*. Oxford: Rowman & Littlefield, ch. 9.
20 Wittgenstein, L. (1953) *Philosophical Investigations*. Oxford: Blackwell, Part II, p. 207.
21 Wittgenstein, op. cit., note 20, para. 242.
22 Wittgenstein, op. cit., note 20, paras 150–6.
23 See J.L. Austin (1961) Performance utterances, in *Philosophical Papers*. Oxford: Clarendon Press. The theory is developed more fully by John Searle (1969) in *Speech-Acts*. Cambridge: Cambridge University Press.
24 Geertz, op. cit., note 18, p. 136.
25 Geertz's definition in *The Interpretation of Cultures* (1975). London: Hutchinson, p. 445.

Biographical notes on contributors

Wilfred Carr is professor of education in the School of Education at the University of Sheffield. His main research interests are in the philosophy of education, educational theory and educational research methodology. He was the chair of the Philosophy of Education Society of Great Britain from 1996 to 1999 and is currently the executive editor of *Pedagogy, Culture and Society*. He is the author (with Stephen Kemmis) of *Becoming Critical: Education, Knowledge and Action Research* (Falmer, 1986), which was translated into Spanish in 1988 (Martinez Roca); (with Anthony Hartnett) of *Education and the Struggle for Democracy* (Open University Press, 1996) and *For Education: Towards Critical Educational Inquiry* (Open University Press, 1995), which was translated into Spanish in 1996 (Ediciones Morata) and Chinese in 1997 (Lucky White Publishing).

Peter Clough is senior lecturer in inclusive education in the University of Sheffield School of Education. He has written widely on the construction of difficulty in the lives of individuals and institutions, and on the creation of appropriate methods of understanding them. His current occupation is with the legitimation of fiction as a means of enquiry in the social sciences, and he recently published *Narratives and Fictions in Educational Research* (Open University Press, 2002).

Ivor Goodson is professor of education and professional development at the University of East Anglia and at the Margaret Warner Graduate School, University of Rochester (USA). Recent published work includes (with Pat Sikes) *Life History Research in Educational Settings* (Open University Press, 2001) and *Professional Knowledge: Educational Studies and the Teacher* (Open University Press, 2001).

Fred Inglis is professor of cultural studies at Sheffield. After reading English literature at Cambridge, he was for some years an English teacher in secondary schools in Britain and the United States. He subsequently became a reader in the Division of Advanced Studies at the University of Bristol School of Education, and thereafter professor of cultural studies first at Warwick and then at Sheffield. He has been fellow-in-residence at the Humanities Research Centre, Australia National University, Canberra, at the Netherlands Institute for Advanced Study, and a member of the School of Social Science at the Institute for Advanced Study, Princeton, USA. His most recent published works include *Everyday Life and the Cold War* (Basic Books, 1992), *Cultural Studies* (Blackwell, 1993), *Raymond Williams: The Life* (Routledge, 1995), *The Delicious History of the Holiday* (Polity, 2000) and, most recently, *People's Witness: The Journalist in Modern Politics* (Yale University Press, 2002).

Gary McCulloch is professor of education at the University of Sheffield. His recent published work includes *Failing the Ordinary Child? The Theory and Practice of Working Class Secondary Education* (Open University Press, 1998), (with G. Helsby and P. Knight) *The Politics of Professionalism* (Continuum, 2000), and (with William Richardson) *Historical Research in Educational Settings* (Open University Press, 2000). He is currently preparing a book on documentary sources and methods in education and the social sciences.

Jon Nixon is head of the School of Education at the University of Sheffield. Before taking up his current post as professor of educational studies, he held chairs in education at the University of Stirling and Canterbury Christ Church University College. He has written widely on the impact of the new management of education on teacher professionalism within the public sector and on academic professionalism within the university sector. He has also written on the institutional conditions of learning, particularly in relation to contexts of multiple disadvantage. His methodological concerns focus on educational research as a mode of public understanding. He is editor of the academic journal *Teaching in Higher Education*.

Carrie Paechter is a senior lecturer in education at Goldsmiths College, London. Her research interests, which have been developed out of her previous experience as a mathematics teacher in London secondary schools, include the intersection of gender, power and knowledge, the construction of identity, especially with regard to gender, and the processes of curriculum negotiation. She regards herself as a Foucaultian poststructuralist feminist in orientation and writes regularly on issues of research methodology in this context. Her most recent books are *Educating the Other: Gender, Power and Schooling* (Falmer Press, 1998) and *Changing School Subjects: Power, Gender and Curriculum* (Open University Press, 2000).

Richard Pring is professor of educational studies at the University of Oxford and director of the Department. Previously professor of education at Exeter University, lecturer in curriculum studies at the University of London Institute of Education, teacher in London comprehensive schools and assistant principal at the Department of Education. He has recently written *Philosophy of Educational Research* (Continuum, 2000).

Pat Sikes works in the School of Education at the University of Sheffield. She is series editor of the Open University Press series *Doing Qualitative Research in Educational Settings*. She has recently published (with Ivor Goodson) *Life History Research in Educational Settings* (Open University Press, 2001).

Melanie Walker is based in the School of Education at the University of Sheffield. Her research and teaching interests include higher education pedagogies and difference, critical professionalism, gender studies, and languages and practices of deliberative democracy in educational settings. Her interests in research methodologies include action research for equity and educational change and narrative, biographical and feminist approaches. Her most recent book is *Reconstructing Professionalism in University Teaching: Teachers and Learners in Action* (Open University Press, 2001).

Index

access to information, 61, 63
action
  'principles of action', 38
  thought and, 87–91
action research project, university teaching, 92–4
adjustment (adaptation/acquisition), 76–7, 79–81
American Educational Research Association, 52, 54
analytical reflexivity, 102
applied discipline of educational research, 9–10, 14, 106–7, 112
Arendt, H., 33–4, 86, 89, 90, 99–100, 101, 102–3
Aristotle, 13, 99

Ball, S., 20, 33, 43, 111
'banality of evil', 89
Barr, J., 96–8
Bassey, M., 28
Bauman, Z., 89
Bernstein, B., 41, 46, 68, 127–8
biographical approaches
  democratic knowledge-making, 98–9
  narrative study, social suffering, 94–6
  see also life-history approach
Bourdieu, P., 2, 3–4, 41, 68–85, 87, 90, 94, 95–6, 99, 121, 131
Briggs, A., 27
British Educational Research Association (BERA), 28, 29, 52, 54
Brown, R.H., 99, 100–1
Bullough, R., 42

Calvey, D., 52–3, 59, 62
capital, 74, 83
  cultural, 75–6, 79
  symbolic, 69, 82–3
Centre for Applied Research in Education (CARE), 27, 40–1
chance, 73, 74, 75–6, 77, 79
Christians, C., 34–5, 38
club bouncers, *see* undercover bouncer, researcher as
codes of practice, 38
codes of principles/conduct, 48, 52, 54
collaborative approaches, *see* participation
collective memory of researchers, 32, 33, 38, 48–9
  see also life-history approach
Collingwood, R.G., 118, 119
community of researchers, 20, 65–6, 110–11
comprehensive schools system, 39, 45, 46, 47
confidentiality, 59, 62
consequentialist *vs* deontological principles, 59
context, 56
contract researcher, 53–4, 56

contributory disciplines, 25–8, 108, 113–14, 115–16
  eclectic approach, 24, 26–7, 28–9
  educational psychology, 23, 24
  sociology, 41, 45
criticism
  openness to, 64, 65
  self-criticism, 97, 127
cultural capital, 75–6, 79
'curriculum studies', 26

deception
  in research, 52–3, 54–5, 59
  see also truth
deconstructionist perspective, 22–3, 114–15
defence mechanisms, 71–2, 81
deliberation (negotiation), 53, 55–6, 57, 63, 65, 66
  see also democratizing judgement
democratic knowledge-making, 98–9
democratic researcher, 53, 55–6, 66
democratizing judgement, 99–101
d'Entreves, M.P., 100
deontological *vs* consequentialist principles, 59
depoliticization of education, 16
dispositions, 80–1, 99
  'positional suffering', 95
dominated groups, 77–80, 81, 82

eclectic/pluralist approach, 24, 26–7, 28–9
Economic and Social Research Council (ESRC), 1, 42
  Teaching and Learning Research Programme, 19–20
economy of symbolic exchange, 68–9, 71
Eder, K., 98
Education Act (1944), 25, 120
educational psychology, 23, 24
educational purpose of research, 1–2, 4
educational studies *vs* research, 23–9
epistemological issues, 2, 3, 4, 5
expert knowledge, 100

Feinberg, W., 12
feminist research projects, 96–9, 114–15
Finch, J., 21–2
Fine, M. *et al.*, 35, 38
Fuller, S., 101
funding issues, 18–19, 35–6, 53–4

games, 73–4
  of chance, 73, 74, 75–6, 77, 79
  economic, 74
  exclusion from, 78–9
  language, 130
  social, 70–1, 74, 82
Geertz, C., 68–9, 127, 131
gender issues, *see* feminist research projects
goals, 76–7, 121
  deprivation of, among unemployed, 78
  unpredictability and teleology, 88–9
'good society', 13, 14, 16
goodness of educational research, 107–12
  vs utility, 115–16
Goodson, I., 32, 36, 44–7
  and Sikes, P., 33, 36, 40
government-funded research projects, 53–4
grammar schools system, 44, 46, 120–1
'Great Debate', 25, 28
Griffiths, M., 93

Habermas, J., 118–19
habitus, 69, 72–5, 76, 79–81, 83
Hammersley, M., 19, 43, 110, 113, 114
Hargreaves, D., 18–19, 43, 44, 106
Hegelian perspective, 10–15
Heller, A., 88
Higher Education Funding Council (HEFC), 109
Hillage, J. *et al.* (Hillage Report), 19–20, 29, 105, 115
Hirst, P., 25–6, 27
historical perspectives, 2, 3, 4, 7–15, 119–20, 126
  see also life-history approach; social history

horizontal and vertical discourses, 127–8
Humanities Curriculum Project (HCP), 40–1

idealism *vs* materialism, 124–5
individualism, 8
informed consent, 38
institution, rites of, 83–4
institutional frameworks for thought, 87–8, 89–90
institutionalization, 14, 15
intellectual virtues of researcher, 64, 65
'interior reflexivity', 48

Jackson, B. and Marsden, D., 120–1
journals, 27, 28, 29
judgement
  democratizing, 99–101
  see also deliberation (negotiation)

Kant, E., 74, 84, 124
Kerr, J.F., 26
King, M.L., 33–4
Kohlberg, L., 65
Kuhn, T., 34, 121

Lagemann, E.C., 22–3
language, 127–8, 130–1
life-history approach, 33–4, 36–7, 47–9
  researchers, 34–5
    Ivor's story, 44–7
    Pat's story, 39–43
'London School', 27
Lüdtke, A., 81

MacIntyre, A., 37, 88–9, 119
market forces, 35–6, 47, 98
Marxist approach, 14
materialism *vs* idealism, 124–5
mathematics education, girls', 114–15
method/methodology, 1, 2, 4–5
  'rigor'/'relevance' of research, 18, 19, 23–9, 110
  transparency, 110
  see also objectivity, critiques of; subjectivity
Mills, J.S., 60–1
mirror metaphor, 123–4, 125
moment (*zeitgeist*), 35–6
'moral career' of researchers, 47
moral virtues of researchers, 64, 65
Mortimore, P., 107–8, 109
Muller, J., 99

narrative study, social suffering, 94–6
National Association for the Promotion of Social Science (NAPSS), 9
National Association for Teaching About Race Relations (NARTAR), 41
National Educational Research Forum (NERF), 19–20, 29
negotiation, *see* deliberation (negotiation); democratizing judgement
Newcastle Report, 9
Niemöller, M., 33–4
non-empirical work, 106–7
Nora, P., 49
Nussbaum, M., 88

objectivity, critiques of, 69–72
  quantitative *vs* qualitative research, 21–2, 42, 122–3
  scientific positivism, 118–19, 121, 122, 123–4, 128–9
  see also subjectivity

Parks, R., 33–4
participation, 90–1, 93–4, 98–9
Pascal, B., 70, 72–3, 82
Peters, R., 14, 24–5, 27
Plato, 12, 13, 76, 77
pluralist/eclectic approach, 24, 26–7, 28–9
policy and research, 113
political issues
  context of research, 53–4, 56
  depoliticization of education, 16
'positional suffering', 95
positivism, 118–19, 121, 122, 123–4, 128–9

power
  dominated groups, 77–80, 81, 82
  and gender, *see* feminist research projects
  and participation in research, 90–1, 93–4
  researchers and researched, 96, 102
  rites of institution, 83–4
  see also capital
'practical philosophy', 13, 14, 15, 16
practice
  applied discipline, 9–10, 14, 106–7, 112
  codes of, 38
  life-history approach, 47–8
  moral, 37–8
  see also thoughtful research
principles, 52, 54, 56
  conflicting, 59–63, 65
  consequentialist *vs* deontological, 59
  'principles of action', 38
  'rules' and, 58
  see also respect
Pring, R., 38
profession of researchers, *see* community of researchers
professional thinkers, 87–8
propositionality, 102

quantitative *vs* qualitative research, 21–2, 42, 122–3
'question-and-answer-logic', 119, 121
Quine, W.V.O., 118, 124–5, 126

reflexivity
  analytical, 102
  'interior reflexivity', 48
'relevance', *see* 'rigor'/'relevance' of research
'representative thinking', 89
'reproduction theory', *see* social reproduction
Research Assessment Exercise, 109
researchers
  claims of value neutrality, 48
  collective memory, 32, 33, 38, 48–9
  community, 20, 65–6, 110–11
  examples, 52–7
  'interior reflexivity', 48
  life-history approach, 39–47
  'moral career', 47
  optimism, 32–3
  in the research process, 34–5
  and researched, power relations, 96, 102
  self-criticism, 97, 127
  social identity, 32
  teachers as, 106, 107
  thinking agent-as-researcher, 101
  trustworthiness, 56, 64
  virtues, 61, 62, 63–5
resignation, of dominated groups, 80, 81
resistance, 81
respect
  for persons, 55, 59, 60, 96
  for teachers, 66
right to know, 60–1
right to reply, 63
'rigor'/'relevance' of research, 18, 19, 23–9, 110
rites of institution, 83–4
Rorty, R., 123–5, 126
Rosen, H., 33
Rudduck, J., 40–1
'rules' and principles, 58

Schools Council for the Curriculum and Examinations, 26
Schools Council Humanities Curriculum Project, 27
scientific positivism, 118, 121, 122, 123–4, 128–9
self-criticism, 97, 127
Sellars, W., 125, 126
Sennett, R., 35
'sharing-the-world-with-others', 99–100
Sikes, P., 39–43, 110–11
  et al., 36, 42–3
Simon, B., 18, 25–6
social class, 71, 80, 120–1
  subproletarians (Algerian unemployed), 77, 78–9
  see also social order
social games, 70–1, 74, 82

social history
  the case for, 18–23
  educational studies *vs* research, 23–9
  see also historical perspectives
social identity of researchers, 32
social order, 8, 74, 120
  'positional suffering', 95
  see also social class
social reproduction, 11–12, 14–15, 74
social suffering, narrative study, 94–6
social world, 69–70, 74–5, 77, 82, 95–6
sociology, 41, 45
'sound truth', 68, 70
Spivak, G., 90, 98
state-provided system of schooling, 13–14
statistical analysis, 9, 10
Stenhouse, L., 27, 40–1, 42
subjectivity, 34–5, 36, 47
  and moral deliberation, 63
  'subjective truth', 71
  and value of research, 111–12
  see also objectivity, critiques of
subproletarians (Algerian unemployed), 77, 78–9
symbolic capital, 69, 82–3
symbolic exchange, economy of, 68–9, 71
symbolic violence, 81, 121

Taylor, C., 119, 131
Taylor, W., 25–6
teachers
  as researchers, 106, 107
  respect for, 66
teleology, *see* goals
temporal issues, 73–4, 77–8
theory, value of, 111
Thomas, W. and Znaniecki, F., 42
thought and action, 86, 87–91
thoughtful research, 91–2, 99–103
  examples, 92–9
Tibble, J.W., 14, 25, 26
Tierney, W., 33, 35
Tit[t]ler, R., 48
toilet ethnographer, researcher as, 53, 55
Tomlinson, P., 42
Tooley, J. and Darby, D. (Tooley Report), 19–20, 29, 105
totalitarianism, 89
'traditional subjects', 44, 45, 46–7
trustworthiness of researcher, 56, 64
truth, 60–3, 65
  and social games, 70–1
  'sound truth', 68, 70
  'subjective truth', 71
  see also deception

uncertainty/unpredictability, 61, 89, 93
undercover bouncer, researcher as, 52–3, 54–5, 59
undercover ethnographer, researcher as, 53, 55
university teaching, action research project, 92–4
utilitarianism, 8–9, 10, 59, 60
utility of educational research, 106–7, 112–15
  vs goodness, 115–16

value(s), 35–6, 121–2, 131
  neutrality, 48
  research community, 66
  of theory, 111
  'value for money', 106–7
Verma, G. and Mallick, K., 21
vertical and horizontal discourses, 127–8
violence, 78–9, 81
  symbolic, 81, 121
virtues of researchers, 61, 62, 63–5
virtuous research community, 65–6

Walker, M., 88, 92
Walkerdine, V., 114–15
Weber, M., 75, 82, 83, 122
Whig perspective, 7–10
Willis, P.E., 80
Wilson, J. and Wilson, N., 111–12, 113–14
Wittgenstein, L., 128–30
women's education, 96–9, 114–15

zeitgeist (moment), 35–6

LIFE HISTORY RESEARCH IN EDUCATIONAL SETTINGS
LEARNING FROM LIVES

Ivor Goodson and Pat Sikes

It has long been recognized that life history method has a great deal to offer to those engaged in social research. Indeed, right from the start of the twentieth century, eminent sociologists such as W.I. Thomas, C. Wright Mills and Herbert Blumer have suggested that it is the best, the perfect, approach for studying any aspect of social life. In recent years, life history has become increasingly popular with researchers investigating educational topics of all kinds, including: teachers' perceptions and experiences of different areas of their lives and careers; curriculum and subject development; pedagogical practice; and managerial concerns. *Life History Research in Educational Settings* sets out to explore and consider the various reasons for this popularity and makes the case that the approach has a major and unique contribution to make to understandings of schools, schooling and educational experience, however characterized. The book draws extensively on examples of life history research in order to illustrate theoretical, methodological, ethical and practical issues.

Contents

Introduction – Developing life histories – Techniques for doing life history – What have you got when you've got a life story? – Studying teachers' life histories and professional practice – Life stories and social context: storylines and scripts – Questions of ethics and power in life history research – Confronting the dilemmas – Bibliography – Index.

144pp 0 335 20713 8 (Paperback) 0 335 20714 6 (Hardback)

UNDERSTANDING, DESIGNING AND CONDUCTING QUALITATIVE RESEARCH IN EDUCATION
FRAMING THE PROJECT

John F. Schostak

- How do I get my research off the ground and ensure that it is 'new', 'novel' and 'important'?
- How do I make sense of data, build theories and write a compelling thesis?
- How can my research bring about change?

This book is more than an introduction to doing research – it aims to help readers identify what is new and important about their project, how their research relates to previous work and how it may be used to bring about change at individual, community, national or even international levels. A total strategy is offered focussing on the notion of the 'project' as an organizing framework that ensures that the methods chosen are appropriate to the subject and aim of the study. The intention throughout is to help readers move from being able to apply methods to being able to interrogate the theoretical underpinnings of particular perspectives so that they can feel confident about the particular kinds of knowledge claim they are making. The book will be important reading for students at Masters and doctoral level and will be particularly helpful for professionals from education, health, social work, criminal justice and business who carry out research in their workplace and who need to reflect upon the consequences and possibilities for action and change.

Contents
Introduction – Finding bearings – Subjects: choices and consequences – The other: its objects and objectivity – Handling complexity and uncertainty – Sense and nonsense – braving the postmodern, broaching the novel – Being shy of the truth – Framing texts and evidence: con/texts, intertextuality and rhetoric – Framing ethics and political issues – Framing ethical actions – Writing it – Conclusion – Notes – References – Index.

256pp 0 335 20509 7 (Paperback) 0 335 20510 0 (Hardback)